TRAVELLERS

VOICES OF THE NEW AGE NOMADS

TRAVELLERS

RICHARD LOWE and WILLIAM SHAW

FOURTH ESTATE · *London*

First published in Great Britain in 1993 by
Fourth Estate Limited
289 Westbourne Grove
London W11 2QA

A catalogue record for this book is available from the
British Library.

ISBN 1 85702 140 1

Typeset by York House Typographic Ltd
Printed in Great Britain by Biddles Ltd, Guildford

Contents

Introduction

PERSONS UNKNOWN

Early in December the bailiff came and apologetically tied the notice to a gatepost near the site. Mounted on hardboard, wrapped in clear polythene, the typewritten words are familiar to any traveller. The notice is addressed to 'Persons Unknown'. It instructs the people in occupation of the land to attend the county court. The landowner is named as the local county council. It's the first step in the process of eviction.

The site is the usual mess of vehicles, a winter park-up. A green double-decker looms in the mist, next to a dusty red coach with the words 'Baptist Church' painted on the side by a previous owner. Squeezed in wherever the limited space allows there are a few caravans, an ambulance and several buses. On one of the caravan roofs someone has piled a few bin-liners full of rubbish, out of the way of the dogs. Bits of old car engine lie about turning rusty. A lurcher dog, chained up outside a caravan, looks balefully out at some ramblers who lower their conversation as they pass the site. A couple of absurd-looking Jack Russells skulk under one of the buses. Smoke rises from flues that poke out of holes cut in the top of caravan roofs. The nearest village is a quarter of a mile away.

At the Conservative Party conference in autumn 1992, during the party leader's traditional crusading diatribe about rising crime and falling standards of morality, John Major underlined his determination to deal with 'the illegal occupation of land by so-called "new age travellers".

'You will have seen the pictures on television or in the newspapers,' he said. 'If you live in the West Country and Wales you may have seen it on your own doorstep. Farmers powerless. Crops ruined and livestock killed by people who say they commune with nature, but who have no respect for it when it belongs to others. New age travellers. Not in this age. Not in any age.' Thunderous applause from the party faithful.

'New age travellers', the label given to the thousands of people who live a semi-nomadic life based loosely around the summer festivals, inspire similar outbursts of moral outrage every summer, whenever and wherever they gather in large enough numbers. Once they were simply 'the hippie convoy', now they've attracted a richer, more pejorative vocabulary: they get called crusties, hedge monkeys, brew crew, soap dodgers. They attract hostile, often far-fetched rumours: that the reason why so many of them have dogs is to claim an extra £8 a week social security benefit for food for each one; that last year at Castlemorton some of the 25,000 revellers cooked and ate a horse after it had been knocked down accidentally.

'Persons unknown', the phrase used on the eviction documents that every traveller knows well, says it all. No one even has any idea how many there are. There has never been any serious attempt to count the tens of thousands of people who have chosen this life. Even if you wanted to, it wouldn't be easy.

While many traditional gypsy sites are in towns and cities, most 'new age' travellers like to hide themselves away. Some live in caravans and lorries that you can spot easily, but others live in teepees or benders, lumpy domes made of willow and tarpaulin. Many live in woods, secluded pieces of farmland, or on cliffsides well out of sight, like the couple who live naked in a bender with their child in the middle of a Cornish wood. Few locals know of their existence.

Travellers prefer to remain anonymous. Their domestic

arrangements necessitate breaking the laws of trespass on a regular basis, not to mention countless planning and environmental health regulations. Nearly all of them have at some time transgressed the laws governing social security, vehicle taxation and registration, income tax, unlicensed trading and soft drugs. And the laws are getting tighter. The Department of the Environment is currently drawing up plans to change the section of the 1968 Caravan Sites Act that obliges local authorities to provide sites for 'persons of nomadic habitat' in their areas. If the proposals were put through, squatting on land, which is now merely a civil offence, would become a criminal act.

As a consequence of all this they rarely give more than one name, and the name they give you is often not the one they were born with. They tend to be suspicious of outside interference – it usually means trouble. They feel harassed and misunderstood.

'They say we don't understand them,' said John Major. 'Well, I'm sorry – but if rejecting materialism means destroying the property of others, then I *don't* understand. If "doing your own thing" means exploiting the social security system and sponging off others, then I don't *want* to understand. If alternative values mean a selfish and lawless disregard for others, then I *won't* understand. Let others speak for new age travellers . . . '

In this book, made up of interviews carried out between November 1992 and January 1993, the travellers speak for themselves.

PART ONE

TRUCKS, TRAILERS, TARPS AND TEEPEES

RABBIT

Rabbit is walking his dog through the long grass near the site he's living on near Woodbridge in Suffolk. The site is at the end of the runway at the US airbase, between the perimeter fence and the Scots pine trees of Rendlesham Forest.

The dog is large – half-labrador, half-rottweiler. It had been abandoned in a layby outside Leamington when he found it, all skin and bones with a great big ridiculous-looking head. Now it's a healthy dog. Sometimes, when it snows, the dog pulls Rabbit round on a sledge.

His real name is Peter and he comes from Leicester. They called him Rabbit at school. He started travelling in 1983. He has short, dark, thinning hair and is wearing a tattered black leather jacket that looks too small for him.

As Rabbit walks through the rough ground he's thinking about the 12-volt generator he's going to build that afternoon to light his caravan now that the days are short. At the moment he's using candles. He has found a Flymo, and taken off the petrol engine. What he has to do is mount it opposite the dynamo and join the two with a piece of rubber hose and a couple of jubilee-clips. That way the motor won't shake the dynamo to pieces. Then he'll wire in a regulator box and a warning light, maybe, he thinks, even a voltage gauge, hitch it up to a battery and off he can go.

He sits in his caravan and puts the kettle on. He's a diffident, self-possessed man, with a shy smile. His caravan has few possessions in it. There are a couple of posters by the wall, one for a gig organised by Anti-Fascist Action. 'Was I a member of Anti-Fascist Action? No. It's just a poster. I'm not really a member of *anything.' He grins sheepishly. Somehow the afternoon slips away, sitting in his caravan. He decides he'll make the generator tomorrow.*

I found this caravan I'm in now in a scrap-yard in September '92 for £25. It had been there for ages and nobody wanted it. It's not like a normal caravan, everybody thought it was a hot-dog van or something, because that's what it looked like. But it's not. It's just a caravan. I think it was built by a coach body building firm because it's got an aluminium frame bolted together. It's so solid, I'll never find one as solid as this. At the time I was living under a tarp on the back of a fire engine, a QX, and I was looking for a horse-box to put on the back, but since I got this I'm happy.

I converted it myself and put the stove in. You can get them at auctions, cattle markets and stuff when they're being sold from old workmen's trucks and carriages. You'll pay anything from £20 to £50. And the cooker came out of another caravan. I did have a gas fridge but it took up too much room and I never had too much to put in it. I use powdered milk. I can never get the lumps out of my tea, though. They're like little icebergs.

Before this we were on a site nearby called the Wetfield. It has been a site for years and years. The Wetfield is all right in summer, but in winter it got wet at the bottom of the field and the two tracks turned to rivers of mud.

We got evicted from the Wetfield the first time in November of 1991. It was funny what happened. We went to court and the magistrate came up with the eviction notice. There's no point staying. The day of the eviction we all moved out together off the site, and five miles down the road we found an old abandoned quarry with the gate open so we all pulled up in there and set up camp.

We honestly didn't know anything about who owned the land. It was a complete coincidence. The police came down after a few hours and said: 'You lot think you're clever don't you? You lot think you're bloody smart!'

We didn't know what he was talking about. We said, 'What d'you mean?'

'Because you know who owns this land, don't you?'

'No. It's the first place we came across.'

He said: 'It's only owned by the magistrate who just signed your eviction order from the Wetfield.'

The same magistrate drove down later that night and he was ranting and raving at us. He thought we'd done it deliberately because we knew whose land it was. His missus was even more angry, she came down in a big Range Rover, driving round the site, shining a big spotlight on us. It was about midnight when everybody had gone to bed, but there was this policeman still on site having a look round too with his torch. He walked up to the Range Rover, tapped on the window and told her to stop hassling us.

The next day the magistrate came back, a lot calmer this time, and with a court order.

We moved back on to the Wetfield in June. And then we got evicted again about three weeks ago. It belongs to a Dutchman who lives in Amsterdam. The police couldn't get hold of him so they couldn't get him to evict us. In the end the council evicted us without the owner's permission.

It's not that bad when you get served with a notice. There's a good side to it. Suddenly everyone you haven't seen for ages is outside changing wheels and standing around with their engines in bits and everything gets going.

All the same, I had a bad time when we got evicted that last time. It's only three miles from there to here, if that, but I broke down ten times and the police came up twice.

The first day we got here the Americans at the airbase were worried in case we were CND pulling on. But as soon as they found it was just us locals pulling on they gave us no hassle at all. The other day they were shooting rabbits on the airfield. When they'd finished they threw a load of dead rabbits over the fence for us.

There's loads of fallen wood round here. There's a whole forest that got blown down in the '87 gales. It's only pine which burns really quickly but there's so much of it it doesn't matter. You don't have to go wandering very far and you've got a couple of armfuls.

We use propane for cooking because it freezes at a much lower temperature than butane. I was snowed in in Talley Valley in Wales once for a fortnight. Most travellers pass through there at some point. There's people who've been living in teepees there since the sixties. It snowed so much you couldn't even see where the roads were. We tried digging out the track to the nearest road but gave up because it was filling up behind us. That got really cold. In the morning you'd wake up and the propane would be solid. So you'd get up and get the woodburner going first, then put the gas bottle in the airing cupboard above it to thaw it out. Then you could put the kettle on for a cup of tea.

I can't think of anything else I'd do. I wouldn't mind buying a barn for a while and parking up in there, and getting a job and some more money. I want to get a diesel engine for the lorry so I can go abroad, because with the petrol engine it's not worth it, it uses so much fuel. But to get the engine it means I've got to get the work and to get the work means I've got to get a permanent address. So I've got to find somewhere where I can store this or a farm I can park on. You have to have an address these days or people won't give you a job. I've been for loads of jobs in Woodbridge over the last few years. There was this job I got in a yacht-builders. All they wanted was a lathe-minder to put the bits of wood on and press the button. I told them I'd been a paint-sprayer and they said, 'Good, you can do the painting as well, start Monday. How can we get in touch with you?'

I said, 'I'm living at the Wetfield at Melton.'

He went, 'Oh. We'll let you know then . . . '

I never heard from him again. I even applied for a job at Sizewell. I'm not really into nuclear power or anything like that but it's going to get built whether I'm against it or not. I might as well get some of the money for it. But no chance.

I put all the applications through, but I know a lot of people have applied for work for there from on site and not got jobs. There aren't many places that will give you jobs.

Most of my family think I'm a little bit mad. In fact my father thinks I'm a lot mad. A couple of years ago I went home and went round to see him and the first thing he said was, 'See you're still a tramp then!'

I get on a lot better with him if I only see him for about half an hour every couple of years. My little brother is more what he expects. He's got his own house, his missus, the kids, the mortgage and a good job that he's had since he left school. My step-brother and step-sister have done the same. Only my little sister really understands what I do. I always get the blame for dragging her out into the world on site, but what happened was she'd got kicked out of the house and didn't have anywhere to stay. I had a twenty-foot caravan at the time so I let her stay in there until her and her boyfriend got a council flat.

I think a lot of parents are worried that we're going to drag their children away, but no one's going to make that decision to go on site unless they're not happy with what they've got already. It's not an easy life. It may be quite all right living on a caravan in the middle of summer but it's another thing in the middle of winter.

I never see my family. I should do. I've been meaning to phone my sister for two years, but I just don't like telephones. I can't ever think of anything to say. I wouldn't mind going over and staying for a week, but I don't know. It's nearly two hundred miles and I can't get the rig over there and even if I could there's nowhere to park it. And hitching anywhere from East Anglia is terrible.

CHEN

Chen is a Yorkshireman, a poacher. With his beard and earnest looks he could be in his mid-thirties, but he's only twenty-three. It surprises everybody how young he is. He says the police never believe him when he gives his age. Chen lives with Jane who's six years older than him. They have a two-year-old called Dale, and there's another on the way.

Chen's speciality is breeding lurchers. He trains them, hunts with them, shows them and sells them. The caravan is full of rosettes and cups his dogs have won. Two healthy, big-eyed dogs are tied up outside the caravan and a ferret twists and turns inside a small cage to the right of the caravan's door.

Most days Chen spends three or four hours hunting the steep fields around the traveller site for game, either with the dogs, with his rifle, or by staking a net outside a rabbit hole and sending his ferret in. Some people kill the rabbits by knocking them against the rock, but that's inhumane as far as Chen is concerned. He prefers to grab their front legs in one hand and their rear legs in the other and give a quick sharp tug to sever the spinal cord.

Their caravan is parked up on a small site at Embsay, near Skipton, North Yorkshire, slightly apart from the other vehicles. From the north-facing window you can see up on to the bracken-covered hills of the North Yorkshire moors.

Chen is recovering from an accident that happened yesterday. His arm's still sore. He was jump-starting the double-decker bus that belongs to his friend Decker John when a jump-lead touched metal and the battery blew up in his face, cutting his arm, sending the lid up smack into his head and spraying acid all over his face. At first he thought he'd blinded himself. Luckily Jane

*was there and soaked him straightaway in water so he came off
with only a few small burns. If she hadn't been there with the
water, he doesn't know what would have happened. Today his
arm's still sore but he's done a bit of hunting and is looking after
Dale while she's off in Skipton, fetching water and coal.*

I was born about seven miles from here in a little mill
village. I did a lot of growing up in small villages. Come
sixteen I went to live in Sheffield and spent a couple of
years quite near the town centre. I had a right good taste
of city life, and no, I *don't* like it. I'd much rather be out
here. All the time I was in Sheffield I just used to dream
about all the hills round here. I'd had four or five years of
going dogging round here to remember while I was stuck
in the city.

I learned rabbiting from my father. My dad used to have
a shotgun and used to take me out from when I was about
five or six years old. He used to train gun dogs and he
didn't like lurchers because one of his terriers got killed by
a running dog. But when I was about fifteen a mate of
mine got one from an RSPCA place and we started taking
it out rabbiting. We learned about lurchers as we went
along. At first we didn't know anything about them,
about how you trained them to bring back to hand and
suchlike. We just got them and went into a field and
chased rabbits like raving idiots to start with. But after a
while you get to know the things you can train them to do,
and it saves you a lot of hassle. Now I can go into a field
with my little black dog and just say, 'Away lass!' and
she'll just hunt that field until she finds a rabbit, and if she
kills it, even if she's two miles out of my view, she'll bring
it all the way back to me and put it right in my hand.

So when I was in Sheffield all I could think of was, 'I
want to get back up there. It's a lot more natural than this.'
I met a lad who also had a lurcher and we used to walk
five or six miles to get out of the city centre and find some
fields just to go out dogging, because that's what we're
used to.

It's the people in cities too. You can not know your neighbour for a long, long time, whereas in a village you know everyone. I didn't like it, me. I was living right across from the big high-rise in Sheffield, Kelvin Flats – a shit-hole. I got a lot of hassle from up there. I met a girl in Sheffield and her previous boyfriend was from Kelvin and they were all forming gangs and all that sort of shit. It were crap.

I thought, bugger that, and moved back up here. I moved into a farmhouse. That was the first step to becoming a traveller – about ten of us renting a farmhouse together quite near here. Three lads rented it in the first place and another seven of us moved in, but it was all right. We worked for the landlord, paid our rent and it was a great place.

We'd been to a few festivals and that and they had been really nice places to be, so we decided that we wanted to do it. The first festival was Ribblehead in 1987, up under the viaduct there. It wasn't big. At the peak of the weekend there were only about a hundred and fifty to two hundred people up there, but it was a really nice festival. Everything went off so free and easy, and that's what really made us say, right, we're going for this. The next year there, there was about a thousand travellers, let alone everyone else. There must have been about two thousand people there. It had normally been a very quiet little festival that.

We just decided that we wanted to get a van together so a few of us left and went on the road. I went into a caravan site owned by a gypsy and rented a caravan off him for a while to get a taste of caravans and suchlike. Me and Jane met on that site. We went ont' road from there about three years ago. When we left that caravan site we travelled in a little Ford Escort van with three dogs, sleeping int' back on a couple of quilts chucked down on the metal and a woodburner in there as well! It was quite cramped. And we've just gone on and gone on from there. It can average out at about ten cars a year, me and Jane. We like to change. Just about every van we've had the Social's paid for it with loans – we had to pay them back of course.

I'm always out rabbiting, me. We take our lurchers right seriously. We take them to shows, we've got rosettes and cups. At the moment we've got two, but we've had up to six. We breed and sell a lot of pups. There are a lot of top breeders in England now who buy pups off me and my brother, who lives down in Skipton. Both of us got into lurchers at the same time and we've carried on breeding off our own dogs, and we can sell dogs for a considerable amount of money – been offered up to £500 for one dog. My brother's just won the Cumbrian championships with a bitch that we bred. That was dogs from England, Ireland, Scotland and Wales. He takes showing a bit more seriously than me – I do a bit more going out rabbiting.

We started the fad off with lurchers around here. There weren't many at all at first and it just grew and grew and grew. The thing is, they all got them with the attitude that they wouldn't have to feed them because they just catch rabbits, but it's a bad attitude because they go out into the fields and they end up getting shot because they do start taking sheep 'cos it's loads easier. Sheep are stupid, but it takes a cunning dog to catch a hare.

A lot of 'new age' travellers think that dogs are free spirits and should be left to do what they want. Well personally I think that's crap, because the farmers have to make their living whether we like it or not and sheep is their living. Our dogs are tied up. They're let off for a run and for work, but a lot of people leave theirs off continuously. We've just lost a terrier because someone else left theirs off while she was in heat. It was a bigger dog, a collie, and it got on to her and ruined her inside, ripped all her insides to pieces and she had to be put down.

That's just callousness. The owner felt his dog shouldn't be tied up because he was a free spirit.

Travellers' dogs do kill sheep. It happens. They get worried to death, they get ripped to death, lambs get taken. If a dog goes hungry for longer than three days its natural instinct is to chase something.

We've had farmers round here who've had their sheep worried and they know it's not ours because they've seen them chained up every day and they've seen us on the fields, working them for rabbits. Some farmers don't mind us working their fields, most of them do, though. In France you can hunt anywhere, but in England they just won't have it. They'd rather use summat horrible like myxomatosis. And they've just come up with a new disease because rabbits have become immune to myxy.

Not so far from here you've got the Duke of Devonshire's land and there's rabbits everywhere. I don't know why he just doesn't let us keep his rabbits down, because myxomatosis hasn't stopped them. They've just been tortured for the last fifteen years. Their hair drops out. You can tell the ones that have had it, because they're all bald around the eyes. They're all right to eat, though, it's just like catching flu for them now.

We lived on the Duke of Devonshire's land for a while. He owns a lot of round here. I had gone out with the dogs and I got two or three rabbits on his land and I was just on my way back to where the caravan was ont' moor and I spied a policeman's helmet just sticking out above a wall and thought, 'Hey up!' So I hid these rabbits in a drain and I thought the best thing to do was to walk straight up to the policeman and totally deny I'd been poaching. I walked up to the wall and just went, 'Boo!'

He jumped up and said, 'You're under arrest on suspicion of poaching.'

I said, 'Well I haven't got any rabbits.' But no sooner had I said that than his walkie-talkie went crackle-crackle: 'We've got his rabbits. He left them in a drain.' The gamekeeper who had got the police out after us was calling through on it. He'd been walking behind me all the time and I hadn't sussed it! He must have seen me hiding them.

The police told me they were going to put a summons out for me poaching. Now we'd met the estate manager there before. He came to visit us before Dale was born and he's come in and had cups of tea. He came round to us a couple of days after we'd been caught by the police and told us the Duke of Devonshire has a lifetime eviction for that moor, so he can evict anybody. 'Fair enough,' I said, 'but what about poaching the rabbits?' The manager, who's a nice guy, said if we moved off the moor on to a layby they'll forget the whole thing. We moved, straightaway.

But I know a lot of people who've been done for poaching on the Duke of Devonshire's land and have done time for it and had their dogs destroyed.

We've just been given permission to go and live on the edge of 2,000 acres of land and hunt that land, hare, deer and pheasant. Jack Mellings, the landowner, met us when I was out poaching on his land and Jane was out picking magic mushrooms. So of course I hid behind the wall and Jane carried on picking them because they'd already seen her. And he said, 'Oh, you can pick all the mushrooms you like, love.' He's eighty-odd years old. Didn't think anything about it until this year when we went to a dog show on his land and he goes, 'I remember you. And I know they weren't eating mushrooms you were picking, ha ha ha!' Then we got talking about dogs, because he'd seen us at various dog shows and that and he said, 'Well, I've got a bit of land up there that'll fit your caravan on it nicely and if you want to go out and catch a rabbit or a hare or two, then do what you do.'

We've got permission for that, but we're leaving it for an emergency. In winter it's good to be parked up some-where where you know where the water is. If we're skint we've always got a meal in our bellies from my parents. It's nice to be near family in the winter. In summer we like to travel. This one's due in March, so come April we'll be gone. We're doing Scotland this year.

But now it's winter and we're parked up near a town. Towns are usually bastards to travellers. Villages are better. Farmers'll come up and say, 'Why haven't you introduced yourself round the village? How are you? Want some milk for the kids?' That freaks us. We're more used to fuck-off looks from people.

There's a big difference between town police and village police too. Village police are sound. We've had village police that are that sociable we've wanted to ask them in for a drink. I wouldn't ask any town police in, ever. Town police come up and say, 'What are you doin' here?'

But round here it's pretty good in other ways. Skipton's a good Social. They give you your giro, they don't give you hassle. A lot of places will make you sign daily. Some of them that we went to down south this summer we ended up having to sign on at Boston, which was forty miles from where we were parked and they wanted us to sign daily, but the money they were offering just wouldn't even cover the cost of getting there.

And round here we can go out hunting rabbits, hares, deers, pheasants. And at the same time you don't have to do much shopping because they've got a good skip in Tescos in Skipton. And they throw a lot of stuff that's out-of-date in there – and a lot of stuff that's *not* out-of-date, a lot of stuff that's perfect, it's just damaged packaging. They've been all right about us skipping until recently. Now they've started bolting them up and suchlike. People still go down, though, they just take a blowtorch with them to cut the lock off. The amount of locks that has been on that skip is unbelievable. Imagine chucking food away when there is people who don't mind eating it – 'cos I don't. You can smell it if it's off. Most of what you get is tinned things that are just dented anyway, or stuff that's just defrosted and they can't refreeze it. It's literally thousands of pounds every day from each supermarket goes into them skips. Morrisons has security guards to watch their skips. Some put spiked fences all around their skips. It's crazy.

It's getting harder to get water around here too. At one point most every petrol station we went to would let you get it, but now, no. The main petrol station everybody uses won't. We used to go to Morrisons, the big supermarket in Skipton, they have a big car-wash place and there's a tap there, but they've started to stop us using it.

They say they're on a meter. We've offered to pay, but as far as they're concerned, that's not the point. We usually fill up three or four water carriers when we go for a bath round at our parents. The garage at Embsay's all right, but he likes you to fill up with a bit of petrol if you're going to use his water, which is fair enough because he's on meter as well. He's been good to us.

With kids you're a lot more accepted. Before we were just 'crazy new age travellers'. We used to get cars driving past beeping horns. We still do here, because it's a big site near a town. When we were just 'new age travellers' people were very wary, but now Dale's come along and there's a few kiddies' toys outside, and they see him and they see he's doing well it's easier. They might say this isn't a good place to bring a child up, but personally I think it's a better place than in a town.

If you're in a town it's a case of doing what the other kids are doing. You're a poof if you don't smoke. They don't get that. I think site kids are brighter. They're a lot more conscious than town kids and village kids. Dale's only two years old but he helps me every day.

My dad never stops commenting on how well Dale is. He's really amazed that Dale's so bright. I don't know what they were expecting, but at first it was all, 'Well, what are you going to do? How are you going to get a house? How are you going to settle down? You can't carry on like this.'

At one point they wouldn't even come and see us, but when Dale was born they wanted to see their grandson. Now they come on to site at any time, anywhere, no matter whether it's ten vehicles or a hundred. They don't care now. They know a lot more about it. It's opened their minds up about travellers a lot too.

Me and Jane like our privacy. Sometimes we just go and park up on our own. We don't like big sites. Last winter, when we were here on our own, there was a big site over at Linton we went to visit. It was an illegal site. Originally we found it for them, as a matter of fact. There were a lot of people round here and they needed somewhere to park, and there had been a lot of police hassle. So we went out, me, Jane, a bloke called Dave the Rave and we pulled up on it and thought, yeah, this is a good place. It ended up that there were over eighty vehicles on there and a couple of hundred people. It was a massive site. And there were roads on the site and they had names like Toxic Waste Avenue and Dave the Rave's Square. Dave is another lad I grew up with and we all got vans together and that, from the start. He's quite a hyperactive person and that. He has a sound system and plays rave music. We really like each other but if we live together for too long it just blows. There were a lot of good people on the site at Linton but there were a lot of junkies as well and needles were being left laying around. Personally that really annoys me because there were children about.

There's some good people on this site and we know everyone. A lot of us here have lived together for quite a lot of years in various places. There's people on here that I've grown up with. We all help each other. If someone's without a car we help fetch them water. It's really good. There aren't any junkies here.

What's going to happen round here is this whole area is going to be designated under the 1968 Caravan Sites Act and the council are going to give us a site, which we don't want. Me and Jane have always been against being given a permanent site. You're no longer travellers, just designated to one place. You can't go and park where you want to park.

It would just stop everything we've tried to achieve.

SCOTT

Scott and Jane are committed townies. There're more shops, more facilities, more going on and more rubbish. They make their living out of stuff people chuck away – either scrap metal which they can sell for recycling or junk that they move for people on their flat-bed lorry.

Living in town makes it hard to keep a site for too long, though. It's hard to tuck yourself away out of sight in the city. There's more people's noses to get up.

Scott and Jane have got used to it, learned to be brazen and cheeky. They once parked on Chris Eubank's land. He was quite nice about it – went to talk to them personally, was interested in their situation and gave them a few days to find somewhere new. The Hells Angels, All England Chapter, whose land they squatted in Surrey were nearly as polite; they gave them a bit of time. But the word 'bloodshed' cropped up in close association with the words 'two days' time'.

They've just been evicted from a site on British Rail land next to Brighton station, but they've found themselves quite a good new spot in the yard of a derelict Co-op Dairy.

They're not sure if it'll last. But if it doesn't, something will turn up. It always has in the past. Scott's been travelling since 1984, since he left the pleasures of Surrey suburbia for the festival circuit. Jane's been travelling on and off for even longer. She's thirty-six and both her younger brother and younger sister are travellers. Her mum and dad are quite well-to-do. They live in the South of France now but they've got satellite television and they're horrified when they see all the traveller skirmish stories on the news. They keep asking her when she's going to grow up and settle down. At the moment there are no plans.

When I first went out on the road, going to Stonehenge and all the festivals, I didn't think to myself, 'This is great – I'm going to get a lorry and go into the iron business', but that's how it's turned out, really. It's one of the only ways of earning money like this and it's traditional for travellers to do it – gypsies have been doing it for years.

A lot of other people who live on buses and that get fed up in the end of moving from giro to giro and never having any money. Your giro goes in a couple of days – it's very hard to live on £40 a week.

Having the flat-bed lorry means we've been able to work and earn money. Scrap prices are really down and it's difficult at the moment but it was a lot easier a few years ago when we started. When it was booming you'd get about £35 a ton on average and you could easily get a ton to two ton on a good day. These days you're lucky to get £35 for two ton. It's just the recession really.

We do rubbish as well, just going round clearing rubbish for people. You can maybe make about £40 a day. You just drive round looking for piles of rubbish and asking if they want it moved and if they do work out a price. It's got to be an amount that people wouldn't think it was worth getting a skip in for.

There's money in that still but there's this new licence that's come out. It's ninety quid for three years, which is cheap, bugger all really, but if you're signing on and not paying taxes it causes problems. We haven't got it yet because we thought that maybe we'd get ourselves in some deep water if we did. So carrying rubbish on the road is illegal now and at the dump they won't let you dump it if you haven't got a licence. But we'll get back into it soon.

Scrap's a good business once you get established. You start off by driving round looking for it. After a while when you're known for it, people give you jobs, get in touch with you when they want to get rid of stuff. And there's always places you can find scrap. You've just to think of the places where they're likely to have scrap iron lying around like garages, exhaust centres, domestic appliance centres where they service washing machines. You've got to know the ropes a bit to know how to do it but it's quite easy once you know how.

If you stick at it in one area you get to the point when you get up in the morning and it's just there waiting for you. You'll have three or four calls you've arranged to make. We used to have regular places to visit and whenever we didn't and wanted to get a quick load we'd go to council estates – they're always good for scrap. You can either just drive around looking or call for it, shout out 'Any old iron'. You get a good sort of mix of scrap and there's a lot of it, because it's a high concentration of houses all in rows. You get irons, washing machines, cast-iron baths, everything. People in council estates when they get a new cooker are more likely to just dump the old one in the garden and forget about it. In posh places they're more likely to get rid of it straightaway. And blokes muck about with cars and that, so there's always old bits of scrap from cars. All in all you get a better class of scrap in a council estate than in a posh place.

Scrap's a good little business. It's worked for us. We've earned enough money over the last seven years to give us a fairly comfortable life. Everything we've got here is through scrap, basically.

It means we've got more to lose now when it comes to festivals and things, trouble with the police. We got a bit pissed off with the festivals last summer. We were at that Torpedo Town place, a festival on the site of an old arms factory, and we were next to that recycling centre when it got burned down. Some bloke got a bulldozer and broke it open and people went in painting graffiti everywhere, nicking stuff like gas bottles, burning it down. That put us off really. I don't want to get involved in situations like that. We've got a lorry that's worth a grand, a trailer that's worth a grand, all our possessions, and we don't want everything damaged. I've been through the Beanfield, Stoney Cross, all that and I don't really want it all again.

We've matured a bit. It's nine years later. When I went on the road I had different attitudes. When you get a bit older you want to get your life together a bit, earn some money, have some home comforts.

We like having nice things. Jane buys a lot of china, ornaments, clothes and we've always had a lot of books. We don't live much differently from people in a house except we can move when we want to.

People get the idea that if you live in a trailer you're roughing it. They think you get cold in the winter. They're really surprised you've got a video. They think you sit there shivering in a blanket, munching carrots all winter. But we live as comfortably as anyone in a house.

We'll probably get a mobile phone soon, get an A- or B-reg lorry and maybe start doing a bit of advertising. Get more into the business side of it and make a bit more money for ourselves. We've managed to save a bit of money in the bank now as well. We've been able to sign on and we don't pay tax. If we were living in a house and we had a lorry going out working, we wouldn't be able to sign on for a start. Sooner or later they'd get us. Because we're travelling they never catch up with us.

The taxman doesn't bother with travellers. They know full well gypsies go out earning money tarmacking and all that but they never bother chasing them up. It's not worth their while. That's worked in our favour.

We bought this trailer a year ago off a gypsy couple we became friends with down in Bristol. We travelled with them for while. I suppose it's quite unusual for people like us to live with gypsies but we got on with them really well.

We both worked the trucks which is how we met. They were doing the rubbish round Bristol and we were doing the scrap. If they had any scrap they'd put it on to us, if we came across any rubbish we'd put it on to them. Not many of our kind are doing the scrap. A lot of people have flat-beds but they don't really do that much with them.

I remember when we were parked just outside of London near Woking we had the local traveller liaison person come along and she was shocked, couldn't believe hippie types and gypsies living together.

This couple, Sheena and Chris, were twenty-eight, the same as me roughly but they seemed a lot older. Very straight you see. They never touched drugs. They wore really straight clothes. They had their meals at really set times, breakfast in the morning, lunch at half past twelve, evening meal at seven, bed at night at a set time.

Like a lot of gypsies they were very into keeping up with the Joneses. They bought one of those modern gypsy trailers with a slopey front and bubble windows and it was always spotlessly clean. All Sheena seemed to do all day was clean clean clean. She'd go on all the time about all the different cleaning agents and it was a real highlight for her when Jane was cleaning in here. She actually cleaned the trailer for us one day. We don't really clean it very often outside and she hated to see it dirty – because it used to be theirs – and she was out there polishing up the chrome.

When we first got the trailer it was literally gleaming. Their trailers don't really look lived in – they don't really have ornaments or things lying about like we do in here.

They were curious about us and we were curious about them. It was refreshing for us to see a different way of travelling. Us and gypsies all do the same thing, but very differently. And they were really curious about us. They thought we were strange and fascinating. We'd sit with them every night just talking about loads of different things.

They couldn't really understand a lot of things we did, like the music we were into, the books we read. Like that lamp for instance. Their attitude was why use a paraffin lamp when you can just get a generator and have electric light?

They thought our food was well weird. They'd eat burgers and chips, really straight food. We were vegetarians then. Chris would come in and try a bit sometimes and really like it. We influenced them a bit like that. They'd start making proper mixed salad with salad dressing. Chris would make it anyway – Sheena wouldn't touch it.

I think they wanted to change us, actually. They used to say you don't need all these books and everything. They never read anything. She used to give us these nylon pink cushions with light blue flowers on and say, 'Oh, this will go well with your blind' and we'd have to use them.

Even though they were really straight, they swore really badly – their language was really terrible. Even the youngest kid, Jimmy, who was about eighteen months, swore and he couldn't even talk.

They had some funny ideas. While we were travelling with them, their little girl Kelly was about five or six and he was already saving up for her wedding. And when the boys were seventeen and could drive they were both going to be bought flat-bed trucks, so he was saving for that as well. Obviously before that they'd be working with their old man, shown the ropes, shown how to go out with a truck and earn money. All they'd need was the truck and they'd earn money.

And the girl would get bought a wedding. We'd say, 'Maybe Kelly will want a flat-bed truck like her brothers', and they couldn't get their head round that. They said, 'No, no, no, Kelly will find a hard-working man, not some long-haired layabout, and he'll look after her.'

The gypsy ways are odd. Like when they sold this truck to us we didn't just hand over the money and that was it, it was like this formal handing over. And he said 'We wish you all the luck and happiness we had in this trailer, we hope you enjoy it as much as we have.' I mean, they'd only had it for a few months.

Although we were so different we got on really well. They were really nice people, real characters. They left to go to Appleby fair, the biggest gypsy fair in the country, but we've arranged to meet them again in the spring at Stowe fair so we'll maybe travel with them again. We've got it nice in here now – nice trailer, nice size. We're very comfortable, like middle-class travellers I suppose. But we'd like to go abroad for a while. We want to go to India and the Far East, ditch the trailer for a while and travel. That's what we're saving money for. We'll see what happens, take it as it comes.

ALEX

*Today Alex has taken the day off work. Jas is away at the factory
in Penzance, but Alex has stayed tucked under the duvet reading
Tank Girl strips in* Deadline *at the back of their large Panorama
bus. It's parked up on the cliffs near Land's End, among a
handful of other vehicles. There's an Aga stove halfway down,
unlit. Two black kittens crawl over him. There are spider plants
dangling in macramé plant-holders.*

*Most mornings he would be up while it was still dark, driving
Jas to the factory, then showing his face at the agency. Most days
they give him work in the fields nearby, cutting cabbages or
broccoli. Later in the day he'll get a lift into town and pick
through the skips for some wood, but right now it's midday, and
the bed is warm, and things could be worse.*

My parents had done the property thing, buying
dilapidated farmhouses, doing them up and selling
them. The eighties' dream worked very well for them. My
father's a solicitor and they got pretty much where they
wanted to be, and they lived on a farm in Hertfordshire. I
lived in a caravan on the farm because they didn't want
me round the place smoking what I was smoking and
messing up people's heads with the general atmosphere.

When I was seventeen I went and lived in Wales for a
while, in Talley Valley, Teepee Valley. First I stayed with a
guy for a while in a teepee, then I bought my own for £80.
It's the poles that are expensive. I can't remember how
many, about eight, but the number is spiritual. They're

Sioux teepees. The idea was to get taught to make them and then make my own, but I didn't quite get it together.

They're pretty hard wearing, unless you've got a dodgy one like I had. You've actually got an open fire inside in the centre and you've got smoke flaps at the top, but it takes quite a while to get it comfortable. You can be living in one a long time before you learn how to do it. I didn't find it easy getting the hang of the smoke flaps. I spent a lot of time in the corner huddled under a blanket trying to keep away from the smoke. In the winter you build what's called a half-zone inside it, which is basically a bender inside the teepee for double insulation. In the summer it's blissful, you can roll the sides up around the poles and you're sitting in the field.

There's something pretty magnificent about the sight of a load of teepees stuck together. In Talley, people were split at the time. There's the centre village, with about twenty people in it, which has been there for a long time and is pretty much self-sufficient. But there was a lot of friction between the centre village and the people on the outside where there were vehicles and first-time teepee dwellers and a lot of people with romantic ideas of what it was going to be like. Although it's communally owned, the council are trying to tell them they haven't got residential planning and they picked up more trouble when vehicles started turning up, which is understandable. If you go there and walk into the middle, it's lovely, but if you walk towards the outside there's bags of rubbish, just left lying around, and more shit around.

I lived there until the hurricanes came. Most of the teepees didn't get touched, but mine was slightly substandard. It didn't really last the hurricanes too well. I wasn't there at the time, I was down visiting my girlfriend, but when I came back nothing had happened to the majority of the teepees, but there was very little left of mine. My belongings were everywhere. So I went back to the caravan and got a job as a roofer after that because all of a sudden there were all these houses without any roofs on. I earned myself about a thousand pounds and then got a ticket to Africa.

I went to Zimbabwe and hitched round for a while. I didn't like England very much and in contrast it seemed like paradise. Loads of fruit and weed basically. I got into smoking a lot. Over here if you're into that you tend to tailor your entire lifestyle around it, because it's dangerous and it's expensive. There it's virtually free and available. I thought that was great. I spent the first few months attempting to smoke as much good bud as I possibly could. When that wore off it just became part of life, which was an excellent process, because it wasn't the driving force in my life any more.

I went to Malawi with four other people I'd met. I had the best time of my life. There was a lot of death, which I found hard to handle at the start, because it's so close and touchable and so hard and fast. You get used to that, it's all part of life, but here people have such a terror of it. We were staying at an incredible beach house in Malawi on a two-mile-long patch of white sand. One day we had been out on the beach, just relaxing and smoking the local Malawian smoking tools. We couldn't walk too well, but we managed to crawl our way back to where we were staying. There was an American guy with us and he was walking about four hundred yards ahead, then he stopped. When we caught up with him he was just staring at the sea, saying, 'Look, Look!' We just thought he had been smoking too much. But we looked and just as we did, this guy's head rose up out of the sea and disappeared again. It turned out to be a local fisherman that had drowned. In the end me and another guy plucked up the courage to go and get him and pulled him up the beach. I went to take his pulse 'cos I knew how to give artificial respiration, but I touched his neck and he was rock solid. You could tap him.

We were all a bit shaken, so we sat around him and sang this little song about being a son of mother earth, and returning to the sea and were quite solemn for a little while. Then we had to walk to the local village and fetch his wife and she came back and she was very, very proud. She just said, 'Yes, that is my husband. Thank you for coming to tell me you found him, thank you.' And we just stood there, not knowing what to say. We left after that, we just went away, but it made quite an impression on me. There were numerous examples of that sort of thing. I ended up with a changed view of death. I didn't particularly fear it anyway, and now it just seems like the other side of being alive.

When I came back, my parents' business was in trouble. I moved back into my caravan, and met my girlfriend Jas, and she moved in with me, but when the property boom stopped my father's business started to disintegrate and they got to the point where they had to sell their farm, which meant that I was evicted. We had nowhere to go. So we hunted around for a local site, and there weren't any, and eventually heard of this site down near Penzance. We just sort of thought, 'Right, that's where we'll go.' That was about two years ago, I suppose. The site was called Crowlas, a big site that was evicted about a year ago.

I didn't have a car at the time. In fact my dad towed us down, which meant pulling on was a bit of an ordeal because he drives a Volvo and people were slightly confused because there was this battered old caravan behind this nice shiny car. When we moved on to Crowlas he wanted to take some pictures of the site so he could take them back to show where we were living, so he stomped down the site taking pictures and nearly got killed. Somebody came up with an axe and said, 'Give us that film!'

It was that sort of site. My girlfriend had been quite involved with the rave scene and she'd got very disillusioned with that because of what was happening around London. People were gobbling 'E's and crap acid and it was taking people's brains over. And we pulled on to Crowlas and the first person that came up to us said, 'Nice to see you. What drugs are you into? There's a rave on tonight.'

And we thought, 'Oh no. Surely not.' So we stuck our caravan in the corner. All in all we found the place really nice. We were finding our feet, blissing out on the fact that there were beaches nearby, but at Crowlas there was a Babylon centre in the middle where everything was a bit chaotic. People kept themselves to themselves a bit more round the edges. At the centre there was a lot of Special Brew and 'scrips', prescriptions for methadone, which is something I hadn't seen before and I was a bit shocked by. We both got quite disillusioned by it. I wasn't keen on a lot of the stuff I saw there. There was a lot of domestic violence.

We left before the site got evicted, and tried living at a few other places, but in the end had to go back to Crowlas because we couldn't get on other sites; it was worse than before and there was a lot more heroin coming on from somewhere. I was getting ill by then. For some reason I couldn't keep a single thought together and I was getting depressed and I linked this disillusionment with the travelling scene. So we decided to sell the trailer and try and get a place together. We thought that was the thing to do. Maybe the whole travelling scene was a bit of a dream that wasn't sustainable. Then I sold my caravan to a couple of girls on Crowlas and they disappeared without giving me the hundred quid. That was the last straw. Sod it.

So we had to live in our tatty old Volvo, parked up with a small dog, just outside Penzance. We were really desperate to get a place. Everywhere we went they wanted a large deposit, or they didn't like the look of us, and because we were living in a Volvo, we *were* starting to look a bit dirty. In the end we found this place that was like a chalet on a holiday camp, for about £75 a week, next to Penzance heliport. It was fully furnished, had a living-room and a bathroom and a bedroom. To us, coming out of a car, it seemed like salvation. I can remember my girlfriend saying, 'It's got a breadbin! A breadbin!' And it had a *bath*. We thought, 'Christ, this is what it's about. This is what we've been missing.' It had electricity and a telly.

It was horrible, basically. Our view was other Butlins-type chalets and we had helicopters going over every twenty minutes in the summer. We got into a lot of debt because the housing benefit wouldn't cover all our rent and I got too ill to work. I was messed up. I had deteriorating health, and I was on the verge of nervous collapse. Neither of us knew what was going on. Jas is eighteen now, but she was seventeen at the time. I lost a lot of weight and I had no energy. Eventually I went to the doctor's and said, 'Help. I'm incredibly depressed. I can't get up. This isn't like me, I'm quite an energetic, cheery chappie.'

And the guy said, 'I think you should stop smoking hash and get a part-time job.'

Oh, Christ, I thought, maybe I should. You're in such a state that you believe these people.

I had a vague idea, so I said to him, 'I think this could be bilharzia.' I knew I had been exposed to it in Africa, and I thought either I had something very wrong with me physically, or I was two sandwiches short of a picnic. So I went back and got tested. If I was fully healthy I was obviously a gibbering lunatic.

All the tests came back negative, so I thought, 'Oops. I'm a basket case. That's all there is to it.'

It was a vicious circle. Because you're living with someone you start to wonder whether it's because of that, and that creates emotional resentment, all sorts of things. I tried counselling, going over the reasons why I resented my parents, you know, but after a couple of sessions the woman said I didn't seem particularly messed up.

I was in a right state by this time. I figured I was HIV and I had AIDS, and this and that. What saved me was one day my parents came down to visit and my mum took one look and said, 'In the car. You're in trouble.' And she drove me straight to the Hospital for Tropical Diseases in London. They tested me and said, 'You're shot through with bilharzia.' The tests in Penzance had come back negative because they didn't have facilities to detect it in the pathology labs there.

They treated me and that was a simple fix. Four or five big heavy horse-tranquilliser-type pills and I started to come back together. The way it's been explained to me is that it's a parasite, and all the eggs collect at the top of your spinal column and mess up your thought patterns.

With the return of my health, I started to look at exactly where we were living. We had both been trying to kid ourselves for a long time that we were doing the right thing. We were turning ourselves into proper people. I have a need for respect and to be considered a valid human and the idea they churn out is that to do that you have to have a proper place to live, and you have to have a job. The place we were living was more like a low-grade mental asylum than a housing estate, where everyone like that ended up, and nobody spoke to each other. One woman used to walk up and down outside our house all the time, peering in the windows. We got burgled a few times and generally made ourselves very unhappy.

After six or seven months there we looked at each other and we both cracked. 'Oh my God, thank Christ for that. I hate this place too. We've got to go back on the road.'

The toilet was doing our fucking heads in. We worked out how much water we used every time we flushed the toilet. The stuff was fucking drinking water, pure drinking water. Five gallons of water every time you flushed. On site a five-gallon water-butt is heavy. You can only carry two at once and you have to put them down every hundred yards. And a toilet is using one of those up every time you flush it. We tried flushing it once a week, but that didn't work.

As soon as we made the decision Jas turned eighteen. She got £500 for her birthday and her gran died and left her £500 in her will. There was a coach company right opposite us, so we went over there and noticed a coach that had been used as a school bus, but was going to be sold for scrap. We offered him scrap value and he charged us a little bit more, £1,200, so we sold a stereo for £300, bought it, piled our stuff in and set off.

If you're renting, you get say £30 a week dole and say £40 a week in housing benefit. That's £70 a week. So if you are going to find a job it's got to be about £100 a week to cover that and the costs of getting to work and so on, which isn't very easy to do here. In a bus I can work a lot more and I'm a lot better off than I was. It's not difficult to earn £30 a week so I'm far more motivated to work. My girlfriend works in a factory in Penzance where she earns £79 a week for forty hours. I'm working on the broccoli and the cauliflowers and if I'm lucky I can make £38 a day working flat out. So it's got us out of the poverty trap.

This is a selective site. It's a bit fascist, not a lot of people can come on. This site's a supportive network that actually works. Everyone's living together.

In town we got so out of touch we didn't go out, we didn't go anywhere, just spent all our time watching telly. You just forget what it's about. We spent the first three months here in a constant state of screaming enjoyment. Summer up here was incredible. There's a rock pool which fills up at high tide and it's exposed at low tide. It's thirty foot across and twenty foot deep. We swapped a view of prefabs and helicopters taking off every twenty minutes, which was mind-blowingly noisy, for a view of uninterrupted, unspoiled coast and a view straight out to sea.

Oh Christ, we're happier now. We've found ourselves again.

LOU

After days of rain the site on the moor above Helston in Cornwall is even muddier than usual. Lou is walking back from a shopping trip in the town with her daughter who's almost two when her little shopping trolley tips and deposits half of her shopping in the mud. With perfect timing, her daughter starts crying. Right then, looking at her muddy cans of beans, listening to Naimh's wails, she has an attack of what she calls straight sickness. 'That's it! I've had enough! What on earth are you doing in a caravan? You need your head looking at, you stupid woman.'

But when she's back on the site in her caravan, the attack passes. The kettle is on, the burner lit, and Naimh is playing with the plastic sheep Lou bought in town. Soon she'll serve up a cup of tea in one of the dainty antique china cups that she's collected on her travels. It's nothing very fancy, just an old converted touring caravan, but Lou and Naimh's caravan is the neatest on the site. There are china plates on the wall. If you see cats or dogs slinking away from Lou's caravan, looking guilty, it's because Lou has bellowed at them for poking their nose in the door and threatening to walk mud on her floor.

Lou is as neat as her caravan. Just because she's a traveller, she doesn't see any point wearing the uniform. She's got an old cardigan on, and a pair of black leggings, but with her gold-rimmed glasses and shoulder-length hair she could be a teacher, or a social worker.

In fact, she was a social worker years ago. And she was a literacy teacher. Her looks and her knowledge of how councils work make her ideal for a job that needs doing. There aren't many places around here to squat and where they live at the moment is

private land. Somebody needs to go to the council offices and get a
peek at the land register to work out which bits of land belong to
the council, because squatting on council land doesn't bother
anybody. And nobody would suspect Lou.
  Brought up in Somerset, she talks with a trace of a West
Country accent. Her daughter's name was a bit of an accident.
Lou thought Naimh was pronounced 'Name-ah', and even
though a Gaelic-speaking friend wrote to correct her that it was
pronounced 'Neeve', the first pronunciation has stuck.

T he man who became my partner, Naimh's dad, was
  travelling in an old Commer van, and rolled by London and said, 'Do you want to come?' So I said, 'All right,
then,' because I was fed up with my job with Southwark
Council.
  I had been a social worker for about seven years. Never,
ever again would I do that job. It was so stressful. I had my
fill of London and the estates around Peckham, Brixton
and Deptford. You're constantly bombarded with people
who are in very difficult circumstances and there are no
resources. The political system doesn't allow for people
who are down on their luck. There were job freezes so
they didn't fill vacancies. I wouldn't go back.
  I gave in my notice, packed up and sold everything. It
was as simple as that. To be honest, I didn't know anything about travellers, apart from having been for years
and years to Pilton, to the Glastonbury Festival. But I
thought, 'Oh well, why not try it? I'll give it a year and if I
don't like it I'll do something else instead.'
  We didn't live with other travellers for a long time. We
travelled round all over England and Scotland on our own
doing seasonal work, at first on organic farms. It was hard
to find the work to begin with. We went round asking
everywhere and got some work through an organisation
called Working Weekends on Organic Farms.
  I remember the first farm we worked on. It was blissful.
We stayed with a community at a place called Canon
Frome Court. They got me to milk goats, which is something I've never done before in my life and the goat kicked

me, kicked the bucket, spilt the milk and wouldn't do what it was told, and it was wonderful. I loved it. I decided that was what I wanted to do. It was so restoring.

So I started on organic farms because I thought we should put our money where our mouth is and support the movement, because I'm very anti-chemical-y and stuff, but because of the labour-intensive nature of the business, they can't afford to pay much. It's not really paid work. You get your park up and you get your meals, but you have to spread out. You start hearing, 'So and so in that county needs pickers', or diggers or whatever.

I've been everywhere on farms, all over England and Scotland, from one end of Wales to the other, and I've done all sorts. The worst was working with this woman's chickens in Cumbria. She was a dreadful stock keeper, appallingly bad at looking after her fowl. She was one of those frightfully middle-class greenies and had read her Jonathon Porritt and Rachel Carson and she knew how horrible pesticides and things were, and she wouldn't give anything non-organic to her chickens. Which meant they were all disease-ridden and had scaley leg and died horribly. And she had a thing about wringing the cockerels' necks, so she had about twenty of them, even though cockerels aren't any good for fertilising eggs, shitting everywhere and waking you up at two o'clock in the morning.

And I did tree planting in the Midlands, which is wet and muddy, but very pleasant. It's hard to explain. Work on the land gives you . . . it's going to sound awfully corny and clichéd, but you get a nice sense of healing. Go and find yourself a nice leek field and hoe that for a couple of days, I can recommend it. It's most restful. Of course, you've got to put up with the weather and when you're picking sprouts at minus something, you think, 'Why aren't I back in London?' But that passes. I wouldn't swap it for anything.

My partner and I split up just before Naimh was born. My ex got the vehicle, I got the caravan. People have been really good, they give you tows, but I'm trying to get the money together for a vehicle because it's a pain having to blag them. You're a bit stuck.

It's very hard for a single woman with a small baby. I was on my own from the time she was born. It actually is very, very hard. People may think it's terribly romantic, but I'd like to tell them it's not. What do you do with a crying baby, when you've got to go out wooding and fetch water? I couldn't do it if it wasn't for other people on sites who say, 'Don't worry, we'll look after her.' But for all that, I wouldn't stop it.

My mother's not exactly enamoured, and my father hasn't spoken to me since I started going out with my ex even though he's nearly sixty and should know better.

But for all that, I wouldn't stop it. The best thing is – this is going to sound so corny – walking out of your trailer on a beautiful clear evening, and being able to see the stars in the sky. It's just simple, really simple.

PETE

Pete couldn't understand what the bin-man was so furious about. There he was waving around what looked like a child's toy that had been left by the bin, a red and yellow plastic bucket, and he's screaming this vicious abuse: 'You lot are disgusting, you're scum, you're fucking animals.' So Pete walks up to him, puzzled, and looks at it more carefully. There's a warning stamped on it: DO NOT THROW AWAY. MUST BE DISPOSED OF BY INCINERATION. It's not a toy at all but a syringe bucket from the local drugs clinic – they provide heroin-users with free syringes; all they have to do is take them back to get clean new ones. Pete can't understand why they can't even get it together to do this. He'd take the used ones back to the clinic himself if he knew what type of needles they wanted.

Living on a site with heroin addicts can be inconvenient. Cans, needles, broken bottles all over the place, the Portaloo provided by Avon Council filled literally to the brim with shit, and now the strong possibility that the bin-men will stop collecting their refuse.

Pete had been surprised when he came back to the site the day before and found that the 'scagheads' had tidied up their area of the site. The site was due to be inspected by the council in the next few days – an untidy site would mean eviction and he was dreading having to herd the scag-users into clearing-up duties. He was baffled by this outbreak of communal responsibility until the penny dropped. The only thing that matters to heroin-users is the next fix; if they have a reliable dealer nearby, it's well worth their while to spend a day tidying the place up to pass the inspection.

Pete has been parked up in this strip of land next to the railway line on the outskirts of his home town of Bath for the last few months. He wants to get his bus properly organised so he can live comfortably as a travelling worker. It's an old Bristol LH401, built in 1974 and in service as a bus in Gloucester until 1986. He bought it off a local football team who'd used it for one season but fancied something swankier when they moved up a division and were happy to use the £500 he paid them for it to buy a new lawnmower. When he got it, it bore the scars of its spell as a team coach – dried vomit in the corners, beer stains everywhere, beer cans all over the seats and the floor half-an-inch deep in fag butts. He's ripped the seats out and transformed it: there's a front door between the entrance and driver's seat area and the main living space, a normal house door cut down by four inches; there's a bedroom at the back; fitted kitchen units; a bathroom with shower and chemical toilet. When he's sorted out the seating area, fitted water barrels over the back wheels and fashioned a bit more storage space, he'll be happy. It has taken three years to get this much done; when he's working there isn't enough time, when he's on the dole there isn't enough money. He's been travelling for three years. After spending five years in the Grenadier Guards he worked as a lorry driver. Then he was convicted of drunken driving and instantly sacked. He took to the road.

W hen it comes to travelling I really am a bit of a baby. Sometimes I think this bus should have a big pink nappy round it. There's blokes you meet travelling who've been doing it for years, some were born on the road, to them it's natural, whereas I have to think about every single thing. It's been a whole new world to me and I've had to learn to adapt.

When I was younger I knew a few travellers. I'd been on a couple of buses and I ran with the convoy round Stonehenge for three months, just for the experience really. That sort of life was something I vaguely knew about and had in the back of my mind.

I was a lorry driver and I got done for drink driving which isn't the greatest of career moves. I was instantly fired. I was in a lot of debt anyway. I got another job, working on an estate in Devon but that didn't last. I didn't know it when I started but the bloke had strong connections with Robert Maxwell and when all the Maxwell shit hit the fan he disappeared overnight. That was the end of the job and it left me even deeper in debt. I decided I could either use what little money I had to pay off my debts and stay at ground zero or use the money to go on the road and work it from there.

The idea was to go on the old-fashioned casual labour route. I didn't have much choice. So far it's worked out OK. Last year I managed to get work for about seven months of the year. I went down to Devon and did daffodil picking, then went on to Wellington in Somerset and did peas, beans, new potatoes. After that it was Berkshire for the straw and hay baling, over to Tiptree in Essex for soft fruit picking for three months, then down to Kent for cider apple picking in the autumn. It can be done, but you've got to prove yourself different from travellers.

When I started I tried to pretend I was a real traveller. But I found that if I went for the gypsy didicoi approach – I tried to pretend I was one – they knew straightaway that I was lying. I didn't know the language, the body language and the nicknames.

Then I tried going in like this lot, the crustie 'new age' types – I put my hair in dreads, didn't wash, all that sort of shit. It sounds silly but it was a completely new field to me and I wanted to fit in without standing out like an absolute dickhead. But if you're a 'new age' type they don't pay you enough and treat you like shit. I found that the best way was just to be completely independent. I live on a bus but it's not your average crustie bus and I'm not your average crustie.

Bath's my home town so I've come back here to stay while I fix up the bus. It's not the most pleasant of sites. We seem to be a regular fixture on the police's drug raid schedule. It's unfortunate. I've checked up on it legally and because it's a motor vehicle there's no way I can stop the Old Bill coming in any time they want with or without a warrant.

I was quite lucky last time because I was awake so I could get to the door before they broke it down. I got up about quarter past seven, chucked a couple of logs in the woodburner, opened it up and went back to bed. As I was sitting on the bed I heard a load of people run past and then another load of people. I thought, I know what that is. I'd just got up to open the door when I heard the bus rock. Then they hammered on the door. I screamed to them to hang on, I was going to open the door. They came in, spent about forty minutes searching.

They're a bit heavy-handed when they come in but once they're in they calm down very quickly. They're very polite, they try to be friendly and I've never had any real damage done apart from the first door I had in between the driver's area and the living area which got kicked in half the first time they came in. I was in bed that time screaming at them to stop.

I was a squaddie for five years so I know what the adrenalin's like when you go in to search a place. You don't know what's on the other side of the door. It could be someone like me, a mellow bloke who just says, 'All right, calm down a minute, what have I got to do?' or it could be some lunatic who's prepared quite literally to die, just to cause you aggro. So I know the moment they come out the back of the van the adrenalin's running. But they do tend to barge in quite heavy-handedly. I mean, what am I going to do? If I was sat on a pound of hash where would I put it? It's a bus. It's got windows and two doors. I can't exactly hide it or bury it.

They've got to do their job; I don't suppose they actually enjoy doing it. I look at it from my point of view; I wouldn't want to go rummaging through someone's dirty laundry and nosing round their kitchen cupboards but that's their job. There's no point in getting pissy with them. It's like when they come on to take vehicles off or to arrest people. I don't actually help them but I'm not actually rude to them like most are. I don't see the point in making it worse. They're stuck in the middle between us

and everyone else and there's no point in making everyone's life a misery. If we all co-operate a bit more I'm sure
we could sort it out.

The people here don't really accept me as a full traveller
and I suppose one of the reasons is things like that,
because I'll talk to a policeman. They don't quite trust me
and treat me as one of their own, but they do respect me I
suppose. I had some diesel and wood nicked once. I went
down and told them if I caught anybody I was going to
break their wrists with a poker. It stopped after that –
nothing's been nicked since. But they do mistrust me a
bit.

With them you're either in or out, it's not as open as it
appears or as they try to make out. Maybe it's also because
I'm a bit older than the people on here – I'm thirty-two
this year, most on here are in their mid-twenties. A lot are
under twenty-one. We had a kid on here earlier this year
who was fourteen. He came over here and sussed out the
site then drove his vehicle across and lived here for three
months. I think the juveniles picked him up in the end.

There's not a thriving social scene on this site. It's not a
pals-y pals-y commune. I think that's more because of the
heroin on here than anything else. But living here, you get
to know people, they come in, you have a chat, have a
smoke and you go down to see them later and they're
totally gouged out. You have to alter the friendship
you've been building up, it's a completely different kettle
of fish. I know that if my life was on the line and they
wanted a gram then the gram would come first. I can't
quite get my head round that really. I was talking to one of
them the other day and I said, 'You're a good person, but
you've got a disgusting habit.' He just looked at me and
said, 'You haven't tried it; if you tried it you'd
understand.'

They're difficult to live with. You get the odd incident,
shall we say. One guy was reputed to be a grass for the
Old Bill. They didn't beat him up which I was quite
surprised about. They just kicked him off – they just said

off you go, leave your stuff here, never come back. They sold his trailer.

There was an incident where some kid, I don't know if it was accidentally or deliberately, got stabbed in the throat. A pretty close call. The stabber knew that if he came back on site he was going to get his head kicked in, so he just left everything. They sold off his possessions, cut his caravan in half with fire axes and then burnt the lot out. As far as they're concerned that bloke no longer exists. They burnt every single bit of evidence that he was ever on site – that's the law and that's it.

I go my own way now, but when I first started I was making more of an effort to fit into the scene if you like. I spent about two years going to as many festivals as I could, more to try and make a buck than to party. You've got to be well-organised to do it and I wasn't organised enough. You have to know where every single festival is going to be, you have to know the size of it and you have to find yourself a supply for whatever it is you're going to sell. If it's soft drinks and fags you need to know a good local cash-and-carry. You have to take it on board as a travelling salesman. I did it by finding out which festivals the drug dealers I knew were going to be at. Then I would do as much work as I could illegally, claim dole and save as much as I could. I'd go down there, buy as much hash as they'd sell me and put it round all the punters.

If you do it fairly, keep your prices down and your weights up, it's quite surprising how much you can get rid of. For me it was, anyway. Obviously, for big dealers it's nothing.

Unfortunately you do have to take a lot of drugs to keep going, because festivals go on for twenty-four hours a day. You blow a great deal of money putting your body back in order after a stint like that, well I did anyway. You have to eat a lot of fresh fruit over a week, two weeks, to get all your levels back up. You need to eat quality food and that costs. But I never made enough money hash dealing to live on and I don't think many people do unless you're doing massive amounts. Maybe it was just me.

Maybe I was being too generous or smoking too much of the stuff myself.

In a way I've found it hard to fit in with travellers, but I'm so used to living on a bus now I find it weird when I stay in a house. My girlfriend had a flat just over the road – she's moved to the other side of the river now – and I tried living in there for a while. I didn't feel comfortable. Traffic noise is different, people noise is different. And living above ground level was a strange thing – going upstairs to bed I was very conscious of being fifteen feet above ground level. You start thinking, 'I can't be feeling the difference in air pressure, there's no way my body subconsciously knows', but I was very aware of the bed, then fifteen feet of air, then the earth. Electricity. I found that I could hear it humming. I mean, I've only been on the road three years and I'm not senile; I know electricity doesn't hum. But I thought I could hear it and I did find it unnerving. Living in a normal building is quite strange when you're not used to it.

You're more aware of the turning of the seasons out here. It's a different space, man – to be hippie-ish about it. I mean, I'm twenty feet from the nearest house and on the edge of the city centre but it's still different. The air's different, not as dry and static; the noises are different – you can hear background noise of town which you don't hear in a house. Maybe it's just me.

I enjoy living in a bus. I just want to get this place as near as I can to a comfortable home. I don't want anything flash. A lot of them completely panel the interior out of tongue-and-groove – it's like living in a matchbox. One I went on in London, the bloke had been round and collected a load of old timber and nailed it all together. He went to Spain, spent three months taking loads of good quality LSD and hand-carved the whole inside – one complete fairytale all the way through. He'd literally taken the LSD, stared at the grain of the wood and carved whatever he saw. Everywhere you looked there'd be a little elf's head or a profile of an elephant or a little scene. I think he must have been a wood butcher of some description because the carving was immaculate and the joinery was pretty good. I won't go that far but I want to get it fixed up like a proper home, so I can have visitors round comfortably, that sort of thing.

Amongst my friends it's the ones who smoke dope and all that, the ones I thought would be more into it, who haven't come over to see me ever. I wonder if they're afraid that it might be all right, that maybe they'd like it and it frightens them that they're quite drawn to being a traveller, one of those oiks they see on the telly. Others have turned up but you can see the uncertainty. They're not sure whether to have a cup of tea in case the cups aren't washed or are contaminated or something. They're not sure whether to sit down in case there's fleas on the seats. I find that quite amusing because my standards haven't changed that much since I was living in a flat. I do have a higher tolerance of muck now, but when you're bringing wood in all the time and when everybody that comes in has to walk up and down a quagmire there isn't much point in sweeping your rugs three times a day. It would just break your heart.

I wear workboots and I wear these thick oilskin jumpers but that's because you have to – when you're out chopping wood and it gets wet you're still warm because it's untreated wool and it retains the heat. Your normal Marks & Spencer's jumper wouldn't last five minutes out here. Some things like that you just adjust to. But once you start doing it and mixing with the people, you find they're no different from normal society in many ways. They have their own standards of hygiene, their own ethics, their own morals. It's a case of having to find out what they are. If you went to live in India or Africa you'd have to shift your ideas slightly and fit in with their ways. That's what you have to do when you become a traveller.

Once I've got the bus fitted out I'll be happy – I can travel round easily, live comfortably and work anywhere. Living like this has made me happier than I've ever been.

I quite enjoyed army life – running round the hills playing soldiers. You're paid well, you're provided for, your accommodation's found and the food's pretty good. You make strong friendships. In the end, though, the constant bullshit gets too much. I got sick of being told how great we were because we were the Grenadier Guards. I got sick of the racism. I'm not a racist person but in the army I'd join in with it. It's just engrained – they'd tell you to clean your boots 'so they shine like a diamond stuck up a nigger's arse'. And then there's death which I obviously came across now and then. It dawns on you gradually that your only value is your willingness to die – that that's what you're there for.

I found normal society more difficult, the way you're supposed to behave: work five days a week and you're supposed to be happy and energetic, two days off where you're supposed to have a good time. Very hectic, very stressful. I'm not lazy, I enjoy working, but I do find it an odd pace to live at. I found it hard to run along with society at that odd pace. Now I'm strolling along at my own pace and it's fine. I don't drink any more, I'm more into the hash. I suppose I've finally unwound.

CHIP

Eleven a.m. It's well below freezing outside on a cold Yorkshire morning and Chip and Floyd have stayed in the bed at the back of the bus as long as they can, but now it's time to get up and feed the kids, Calvin and Rosie. While Floyd stokes up the burner with coal, Chip, dressed in black leggings and a jumper, toasts crumpets for Calvin. She's thin-faced, with long, reddish hair.

Settling on the mattress at the back of their converted coach, Floyd rolls a cigarette, then connects up the tape machine to a 12-volt car battery. Chip lifts her jumper and starts to breastfeed Rosie. Suddenly she stops and sniffs. Something is burning. She looks up at the grill to see if she's left it on. Then she catches sight of smoke pouring out of the back of their brand new ghetto-blaster. 'Floyd!' she shouts. 'Turn it off!'

Of course Floyd's gone and connected up the terminals to the battery wrongly. That's about the third one he's wrecked. Each time they have to take it back to the shop and say, 'We don't know what's wrong with it. We bought it just the other day and it just doesn't work.' Up until now they've usually got a new one without any arguments. Chip waves her hand to shift the thick smoke that's filling the bus. 'Floyd,' she giggles, 'you're a bloody idiot, you.' Typical Floyd. He's always doing things like that. He crashed her car the other day too.

Chip lived on her own in the bus for six months while Floyd was on remand in Armley gaol. They'd been planning to travel to Spain. Instead she ended up living on a site on an industrial estate. She hated that. It's much better up here, parked up near Zed and Chris, Decker John, and Chen and Jane, even if the site is a bit crowded.

Chip used to go out with a musician who dreamed of going on the road. They lived in a council house in Earby and spent three years getting the money together to buy a truck to live in. In the end they bought it with some money Chip inherited.

I t takes a long while before you have the guts to pull on to a site. At first we were just going to festivals. And I used to like staying for a week or two and then I was dying to get home and have a bath. But the bloke I was living with, he was really into it and he wanted to go and do it, and I was sort of, 'Oh no, I want my washing machine and my gas fire.'

When we first got the truck Calvin was a really little, little baby and I found it really hard work. The first festival we went to in the truck it pissed it down the whole time I was there and it was thick mud. I couldn't go out because he was a couple of months old and I had a really, really miserable time. I was never ever going to another festival again in my life. But then he talked me into going to another one in June and it was beautiful, really really hot and sunny and I had a really good time there and that was when I started thinking, well, maybe I could do it. And then we went to Glastonbury and never came back.

I couldn't live in a town, never mind a city. I get paranoid walking round Skipton at night! I can't cope with it. I went to London in the truck once with my ex-boyfriend. He was doing some recording in a studio down there. We parked on the street for about three weeks in Camden, half a mile away from Euston station. They had all parking meters down the street except for the place we were. My boyfriend was recording from eight in the morning till two o'clock in the following morning, and I was there in the truck on my own. One night this bloke followed me home and then another night this BMW motorbike about two parking spaces down from where we were got blown up, and the police were there and the fire engines, and it was just starting to do my head in. It all got on top of me, because I was on my own in this truck and I was freezing and I couldn't light the burner because

I didn't want anyone to know that I was in there. The last straw was one morning I woke up to a pneumatic drill and they were putting a parking meter in there. My boyfriend hadn't finished recording but I went home on the train. I couldn't handle it any more. I was there on my own, just not used to cities at all.

First time I met Floyd was three years ago. He was staying on a site at Gargrave and me and the bloke who I lived with pulled up on the way to the Ribblehead festival. And I've been parked with Floyd ever since then, in a group like.

At first we were just living on the same site, but I ended up living with Floyd in the end. It was the result of various calamities. I was having a bit of a bad time with my boyfriend of the time and I'd had my Mini confiscated earlier by the police. We were moving because the site we were on was dangerous, too near a main road for the kids. We went to pick up the trailer I was living in and the trailer just fell off the back of the truck that was towing it and got smashed to pieces. It just seemed like, 'Oh God!' I had to laugh about it because there was just nothing else you could do.

It was upsetting, but then, after all, it was only a trailer. All me tat was all right. I've had so many different trailers and trucks and buses over the last couple of years that I never get the chance to get attached to them. After that I didn't have anywhere to live. I ended up with Floyd.

Calvin's five in January. I think he likes living on site. He knows loads of people. If somebody new comes on to the site he always knows them a couple of weeks before I do. He goes round and sees them and that. It's difficult now because he's school age and he started in the summer. He went to nursery a bit before that.

The school in Skipton is really really nice about it. When he went to nursery they were nice, but patronisingly nice, you know. 'Oh those poor little traveller children!' Whereas at this school, you do get the feeling they feel sorry for you but not because, 'Oh, you're a poor hippie.' It's more because of everybody else's attitude towards you rather than they're thinking, 'Oh, you poor people, you haven't got a house.'

I think it's easier bringing up kids on site because there's always somebody else that can keep an eye on them if you've got to go and do something for ten minutes.

This site's been here for a while but I didn't want to come here because it's right on the road. A lot of the time we haven't got a clue where we're going to go when we're evicted until the day that we have to go. Then a few people go out in a car looking for anywhere. And we just end up going there. Calvin likes it when we're moving. 'When are we going to get a new garden?' Or you drive past an old site, he goes, 'That's our old garden there, isn't it, mum?'

With kids I can't really move more than ten miles away from Skipton, because legally they're not allowed to carry on going to school in Skipton if we move out of the area. When Calvin first started school we were parked at Clitheroe, which is about twenty miles away, and I had to get up early, well, not that much earlier, but it was a trek to get to Skipton for nine o'clock. But I didn't actually tell the school that we were there, I told them we were parked up here. It's not the school that are the problem, it's the council that says we can't do that, so if we are actually out of the area, like when we were at Steeton, which is actually West Yorkshire, we just lie and say that we're on one of the sites round here.

I reckon Floyd does most of chopping the wood out of us two. I can do it and I have done it but I know that he can do it twice as fast as me so why bother? At first I didn't have a clue how to light a stove or anything me, because I'd had a gas fire all my life. The men will go and mechanic the buses and the women gossip! I don't know about cars, only where to put the oil in. But if I had to learn I would do. Loads of women do know about all that on site. But Floyd can do it and I can't, so that's it.

You get the odd argument. Last week I was going off on one because I happened to be the only one with a car on here and everybody borrows my car. And I came back and I went off on one, 'I'm sick of everybody borrowing my fucking car,' to Floyd. Then I went off and had a spliff and I was all right.

We use the area down the bank by the river as a toilet. I hated it at first, having to go outside. The worst was when we were parked up at Sutton in the rain and snow. You had to dig through the snow to the ground underneath which was frozen anyway. And then when spring came and the snow melted you could tell all the lazy types who hadn't bothered to dig all the way down to the ground. And I must admit last year at Linton, when I was really pregnant with Rosie, I just couldn't be bothered with it. I used to walk down to the toilets in the village.

At festivals they put in those horrible Portaloos. I wouldn't set foot in one. You have to hang from the ceiling or something. No thank you. I'll dig my own hole where no one else has been.

That's always the biggest issue, isn't it? With the ravers and the locals. The locals are always dead worried about our sanitary requirements. We used to have lots of raves at the site at Linton and the ravers would come and they would leave a site in a state of total destruction. But it was just because they didn't know.

A girl would come up and ask where the toilets were. We'd say, 'Outside.'

And then she'd come back and go, 'Well, I've looked all over and I really can't find it.'

'Can't find what?'

'The toilets!'

We'd go, 'Oh, my God.' Dave the Rave, who had the sound system and who used to set up the parties, had a big sign up: 'Dig a hole or shit in your pants.' And a spade next to it. But I think it was really because they didn't understand.

After a while travelling you begin to get the idea of disgust that people actually shit in their own houses. They come up and ask, 'How do you go to the toilet?'

And you say, 'Well, how do you go?'

They say, 'Well, I've got a bog upstairs.'

'You mean you shit in your own house?'

It was hard work with Calvin when we first set out, because he was two and he'd just been potty trained, and he was used to having a toilet to empty it into so that was a bit difficult. But he got used to it.

Then there's all the horrible things like weeing on your bootlaces. I don't suppose that happens to blokes.

LUBI

Lubi, twenty-three, and Toni, twenty-one, are squatting an old quarry site in East Sussex in their pair of army green buses. Lubi's a travelling artist. At the moment she and Toni are working on a community project in Seaford where they're turning a piece of disused land into a garden site, planting trees and digging flowerbeds. She spent the morning working on a Kango, breaking up concrete. After this is finished, Lubi's next job is working on a community art project with foundation art students in Eastbourne in the summer.

Her nose is pierced and she has brown, curly hair and is wearing a large jumper and a pair of baggy jogging pants.

When she was a teenager, her mother and step-father bought a piece of land in Ashdown Forest and they lived there in a caravan for three years. Lubi thinks that may have a lot to do with why she ended up living in buses.

It started when I was at Newport College of Art, in Gwent, making sound sculptures. I make outdoor site-specific sound installations, three-dimensional objects where the shapes are described using fishing lines, to explore the interior space between lines. I'd started making the sculptures at foundation course and then at Newport there's a guy called Peter Appleton who makes sound sculptures who's quite a famous artist.

My sculptures are all electronic. A wind generator makes the electricity that powers the amp and the wind plays on the strings and makes a sound, so it's all wind-generated. I did one once in a park in Newport and it

worked like a beacon. People just walked up to it. When
the wind is really low, it becomes like a guttural sound,
almost like a sleeping lioness, and when the wind picks
up it's like when you rub your finger on crystal glass.
People describe it as being like an angel singing. And
there's loads of wind in Wales, and there's so much song
in what appears to be just a blasting gale.

I got spotted by the arts director for Ebbw Vale Garden
Festival and he asked me if I'd do something up there and
that's when the whole idea came up of living close to the
site where I was working. All my sound sculptures are to
do with creating an atmosphere within a space, and I have
to know the space, obviously.

I've lived in buses for about four years. When I was at
college in Newport, I met travellers through friends in
Bristol. I met a girl called Cara who owned a Commer
walk-through called Molly. At the time I thought, 'Wow.
How can anybody live in buses?' And then I went down
there to see her on the site by the docks in Bristol and I
saw all these other buses, and kids and . . . it was a bit on
the way to Mad Max, especially if you've never seen it
before. I just stepped into the little Commer walk-through
and thought, 'That's it. This is absolutely brilliant. I want
to do this.'

It was the self-containedness. It was all there on four
wheels, and you took your whole home with you,
wherever you went. And that's the thing that really got
me about it. The idea of being completely independent
and 100 per cent mobile, and that you have to reduce
everything you own to fit into your living space. I just
didn't know how beautiful they could be inside as well.
Molly was the first bus I ever went in. They may look a bit
tatty on the outside, but inside they're just little havens.

I bought Molly off her and moved out of a rented flat. I
had to chuck so much stuff out and started living in a
disused outdoor swimming pool complex. Living in a bus
at college you get very well known. 'Oh, you're the girl
who lives in a bus.' But it showed other people that there

were other options than living in mouldy bedsits, paying too much money, and getting ill. The biggest joke was everyone saying, 'Aren't you freezing?' in the winter as you're sitting inside their houses with ice inside the windows. At first I didn't think I would manage any more than one winter. Now I don't think I could ever conceive of going back.

When I bought the bus from Cara, something I noticed was that there were no women who owned their own vehicles. It's incredible. I started to notice that with travellers, men are men and women are women, and men own the vehicles. Because of that the women are reliant on men for a roof over their heads, and such a power play goes on, where women are completely reliant on men for their security. OK, so they don't go around doing the hoovering but they sure as hell are the emotional support systems and they're the ones that get kicked if it's not a good day. They chop wood, but chopping wood is the same as going to Safeways. Quite a few women can fix vehicles, but if at the end of the day it's not their vehicle . . .

In '91 I organised a women's camp in Wales. Part of the reason for setting it up was because there weren't any networks for women. It was a new thing to have a space where women and their children could just get away and get on with living. It's quite dire at times on sites, especially with children.

The site was a place called Pennybank Farm, basically two fields and a short-stay agreement. We set up communal spaces like a purple dome and we had a teepee, and a couple of women from Teepee Valley came along with their teepee too, and we did workshops on issues that women wanted to talk about, abuse of any kind. We set up a recycling point and basically got on with living with each other, doing all the things that you do outdoors. The number of single women who own buses in their own right is growing, but when I first started I only knew of my bus and one owned by a woman called Helen the Hat. At the women's camp last year, in '92, there were at least ten vehicles.

I've joined up with a woman that I knew at art college, we've started up an art company and we've both got buses now. Toni is starting up a ceramics business and she makes amazing clay masks. She's getting stuff together to sell at festivals and in shops.

I've got an ex-army bus now. It's twenty-six feet long with a big bumper on the back which my mountain bike goes on. When I bought it it had all this computer racking in it, and it's got big chunky stabilisers that you drop when you stop, and this notice at the front: 'Height when dish is down, 13 foot 7 inches.' So it must have had a radar dish on the front.

We had to rip all the aluminium computer racking out and convert the bus completely last summer. We found this site and the farmer let us stay on there for a month, and then she let us stay for another month. Now it's got tongue-and-groove wooden floors and cupboards, and I found all my furniture in skips. I've got a low antique pine chest with a sheepskin rug in front of the woodburner. I've got these two bits of 1920s furniture I cut up, one I put the sink into, the other I put the cooker in and I use the rest of it for a cupboard. There's material that billows all the way along the roof and it matches the curtain material and the material on the cushions on the seats. And then we both went out and splashed out on futon mattresses.

The buses are both army green. The trick I learned is not to have Celtic knots painted on the outside. Molly was highly decorated like that, it was beautiful, but I couldn't make it three miles without getting stopped and asked, 'Where are you going? Let's have a look at your documents.' I used to get asked so many questions. It's best not to get noticed. I've got chimneys that go out of the windows now, so you can take them down when you travel, and the windows are tinted so you can't see in.

It's a game of cat-and-mouse with the police. If you make yourself not look like a traveller they're not going to stop you and ask who your auntie is.

In the beginning I was quite inspired by people like Helen the Hat and Cara living in buses. I thought well, yeah, there's something positive I can do for myself and other women. If I can do it, anyone can.

JAY

It's the winters that get to Jay. It's 4.30 in the afternoon and already it's practically pitch dark. It means the kids are stuck indoors messing with the Fisher-Price garage rather than playing outside in a bit of space. It means he can't get on with working on the Subaru four-wheel drive he's fixing up, welding various spare bits and pieces he's had knocking around for years to the complete body shell which he bought last May.

When Jay started out ten years ago he didn't really mind the winter. It was like hibernating, sitting in the van with the woodburner on all day, getting stoned and waiting for the spring to come round. It was a lark then. Now it's a life. He didn't buy a bus and hit the festival trail with a view to becoming an itinerant farm labourer by the time he was thirty, but that's how it has turned out.

Not that Jay's complaining. He's happily settled with his girlfriend Sarah, his two daughters Rowan, who's one and a half, and Rosa, who's two months, his chickens and his Staffordshire bull terrier, Fat Zappa. They were fortunate to find such a settled place to live when Sarah went into hospital to have Rosa. It's in the village of Stretton Grandison in Hereford and Worcester – a spot in the corner of a field on a hop farm with a standpipe, ample space for the two little touring caravans they live in and enough work from the farmer to keep Jay occupied. He's even allowed to park his prized 1970 Volvo in the large driveway of the farmer's house. He likes to keep this in perfect nick and displays it at Volvo-enthusiast rallies.

Sarah came on the road to escape a violent boyfriend she lived with in Birmingham. She went to stay at the Weird Zone, a squat just outside Ludlow, and hasn't looked back since. Jay's been travelling since 1983, a veteran of the 'hippie convoy', the Beanfield – which he talks about in the next chapter, Stoney Cross, the lot. He has a son Laurie who's six and a half and lives with his mother and her new boyfriend in Devon. Jay's looking forward to the school holidays when he'll come to stay with him.

Jay and Sarah have been in Herefordshire for quite a while now. It helps to know the area, to know a few local people. It means Jay gets to hear of the odd bit of work here and there. He gets really angry when he sees signs in shops and pubs saying NO TRAVELLERS. *You even get the odd one that says* NO HOP PICKERS. *He thinks it's rude, and hurtful. He works hard; he doesn't cause any trouble; he just wants to live quietly, to be left alone.*

I wouldn't really say I lived outside society really. I read the newspapers. I follow what's going on in the world. I take a global view of things really and I feel quite sad. I think the world is very wasted by corruption and greed. There is enough here for everybody, it's just that a minority chooses to take such a vast amount of it. The politics of why people starve while others are living in absolute luxury seem more important to me than whether the Tories get in or Labour. It sounds a really terrible thing to say but I actually think this recession is quite a good thing. I think it's only when things get really tough that people look at things more clearly, question the way things are.

And as far as travellers are concerned, we're probably the least affected people in the whole country by recession. I mean we live in a state of permanent recession anyway so it doesn't make a lot of difference. Food's a bit more expensive I suppose, petrol's gone up a bit but apart from that it has no effect. We don't pay the poll tax, anything like that. Everything we buy apart from food and petrol just about is second-hand or traded, the whole black market economy.

The amount of money we have varies a lot. Some weeks I make nothing – there's nothing to do, no work. Other times, hop picking for instance, I earn about £130 a week for working five and a half days. I use money when it's there. I have a bank account so that I can cash cheques. There's an auction local to here that does two auctions a week, one a general tat auction, one a car auction. I was taking stuff up there and they always pay by cheque so I had to get a bank account. I like to keep a small amount of money that I don't need to spend to live on, that I can use to buy things with if something comes up that I might want to buy – either for myself or to sell on. Just a few hundred quid really.

I wouldn't say we live in poverty. I don't sign on. But Sarah gets about £50 a week for her and the two kids, which is enough but it all gets spent, none of that gets saved. We go to town once a week, get that money, put some petrol in the car, do all the laundry for us and the kids. Then we usually spend about thirty-five quid in the supermarket which lasts us for a week. We can get by with that money, but it would be pretty boring without anything extra, money from work or buying and selling. We wouldn't starve without the extra money but even things like putting petrol in the generator would be impossible.

On the whole we're fairly comfortable. We eat quite well. We can afford to drink. We don't go to the pub much though because we've got kids. Because we've got so few solid outgoings – obviously we haven't got a massive mortgage like most people – everything over a very low level is ours to spend on what we want, what economists would call disposable income. From that point of view we have a fairly good standard of living compared to someone with a mortgage earning £300 a week, but then again we still have to tramp quarter of a mile in the pouring rain to shit in the woods. So it's swings and roundabouts really.

Some people couldn't stand living like we do. I don't mind that sort of thing. I couldn't stand living surrounded by concrete. Each to their own really. But I think there is a lot of pressure on people to think they need lots of material things and comforts which maybe they don't really need at all. The eighties was full of that – people having it forced down their throats that they needed things they didn't. You can't have a car more than two years old. You've got to chuck out all your cassettes and buy CDs instead. It's getting as bad as Japan where everything's chucked out after about two months. I can see why people get like that. Everybody has something in life they want to achieve and the obvious thing to go for is material possessions, but I do think a lot of people don't have time to enjoy their lives because it's all spent working, getting money to buy useless things. It's a cliché to talk about the rat race but it's very real and people are caught up in it.

I probably know more people outside of traveller circles than most travellers. There's some people who've got this mentality that everybody outside of this is straight and that's it, we've nothing in common with them. Well that's not true at all. There's people live in houses who are more eccentric than we are. I always find it useful to try and get on with the locals. Here I know more people because I've kept coming back here over the years and I find it useful to cultivate those connections. There's free-thinking people all over the place – it's narrow-minded to think that only people who live on wheels have similar attitudes to yourself.

My parents are happy with what I do. As long as I'm healthy and happy they're pleased. It wasn't a rebellion thing when I first started which I suppose it is for a lot of people. My parents were never strict or uptight or anything, quite liberal really. 'Well-meaning *Guardian* readers against the bomb' sort of people.

My younger brother's got a house, a mortgage and works for British Telecom. He was never a traveller. I suppose he'd always look at what I did and not do the same thing. Different types, I suppose. We get on pretty well but we don't see each other very often – my family all live in Kent and I don't spend much time there. I think his wife's side of the family think it's quite strange though. I remember going to his wedding. Both sides of the family know each other fairly well but none of them had ever met me. So I turn up at the wedding. It was in a church so you get this grading of people in the pews with the immediate family right at the front. I remember thinking I could feel all these people whispering, 'Oh, he must be the brother, the funny one.' I suppose I must have stood out a bit. I didn't have a suit and tie and all that. I had a clean cardigan, a pair of cords and shiny boots. I thought I looked pretty smart.

I've got quite a lot of stuff I've collected over the years – just stuff to make day-to-day life easier. I've got a Honda generator, a compact one, what they call a briefcase one. That's the most expensive thing I've ever bought new: £480. I've got two big battery-chargers that plug into it and two big leisure batteries which are like boat batteries for running television and lights and things. I can run an electric drill, an angle grinder, stuff like that, to work on the vehicles and I can stick it in the car and work some-where else if I get a job on a vehicle for somebody.

We've got a colour television. With remote control which is pretty ridiculous in a place this size but you can't buy tellies without them now. On TV I watch satire stuff. I like sarcasm, dry humour. And at the moment they're repeating all this stuff I used to watch as a kid: 'Thunder-birds', 'Stingray'. I love all that. I don't like schmaltzy American stuff and all those detective things you get all the time, unless they've got interesting period settings which I like. We buy the *Radio Times* every week from the garage and look and see if there's anything worth watch-ing. We don't just turn it on every night and sit there channel-hopping. I suppose we watch on average a couple of hours a night. Lots of travellers don't have tellies though, there's more that don't than do. That's probably why 'The Archers' is so popular. It's a bit of a cult with travellers. It's my soap habit. It features people like us. Craig and Lisa are squatting that cottage at the moment and they're going to be given the tenancy. And they've had people parked up at the Grundys'. I love the Grundys – excellent characters, so funny. The thing is they obviously research it quite well. The people they had

parked up they were going down the shops and buying
Earl Grey tea, which is popular with travellers – one of
those little quirks we have I suppose – and they had
lurcher dogs. The storyline was good and believable.
They'd bought some wood, the right to chop down this
tree, off the Grundys, except it wasn't the Grundys' to sell
and the person who did own it used that to get the police
to throw them all off. Great programme.

I read a lot. All my books are packed away at the
moment in the other caravan. My taste in music and
books are quite open. But you can't keep a lot living in a
caravan. Books are quite heavy as well as bulky – they
don't store well, damp and mice get at them. I suppose
I've got about a hundred books and they range from a
book on the history of Volvo cars to George Borrow,
Lavengro, The Romany Rye, all those novels written in
Victorian times about gypsy life. I'm quite interested in
things related to my own life – I've got a few old books
written by travelling shamen at the turn of the century or
there's one really old gypsy chap, head of a big family, the
stories of their life. I've got a few books to do with the dog,
Staffordshire bull terriers. They're the sort of books I
would keep. Others come and go – I'll read them and pass
them on to someone else, pick something else up. There's
a lot of swapping, but I keep a few. Good books become
like friends don't they, you read them again every few
years. I've got a really old paperback copy of *Brighton Rock*
which I've had since I was at school. I read that every few
years – an evil book but I love it. I read it first when I was
about fourteen or fifteen and there was this interview
with Johnny Rotten in a music paper and he said the only
good thing he got from school was being forced to read
Graham Greene's *Brighton Rock* so I thought I'd read it.
I've read a lot of Graham Greene over the years but that's
the one I've kept.

And I collect china too. That's probably rubbed off from
living with gypsies because they love china and I've been
collecting it for about five years now. It's all packed away
in boxes in the other caravan. I've got two collections: a

Royal Worcester set, hops, plain white with a border of hops in gold leaf round the edge; they've stopped making it now because it only sold in a couple of hop areas, Kent and Herefordshire, and so it's hard to find pieces now. And I collect the Wedgewood Beatrix Potter stuff for the kids. All the practical day-to-day stuff we've got in this caravan here. All the nice things – things to make the place look nice, china and things like that – has all been packed up.

I've got a collection of toy cars, Dinky cars that I've bought over quite a long period of time. If I've had a good week, earned some money, it's nice to be able to spend a bit on something nice. When you live in a small space it's nice if that small space is aesthetically pleasing as well; it's worth spending a bit of money on a few pieces of china or whatever.

The caravan's twenty-two years old – 1970, the same as the Volvo. It cost £400. I bought it from some people who used it as a touring caravan so it needed a bit of conversion. It had never been lived in. It makes quite a lot of difference. Gypsy caravans are built to be lived in permanently – no sink, no toilet, and a far better designed kitchen, all smooth surfaces with no places for the dirt to hide. This is built for people who live in a house just to put a few things into and go off for a week. They tend to deteriorate quicker if they're being lived in full time and that's why they need adapting.

The toilet and shower area is completely useless – would you really want to live full-time in a fourteen-foot place where you crap right next to where you cook? There's no way you'd use something like that if you lived here all the time. The same with the gas fire which again is fine for the odd weekend in the summer but you can't use it all year round. It gets on your chest. The good thing about a woodburner like we've got is that it's very dry heat so it deals with the damp and the condensation as well as the cold. It dries the moisture out of the air whereas gas heating produces moisture. We've taken the wardrobe out to build in those bunks for the kids. We made it look as if it was built that way by using the veneer from the wardrobes and varnishing it all.

We wash up outside in a bowl. I suppose it's something else that's rubbed off from living with gypsies, using different bowls for washing different things. There's two bowls and jugs out there, the bigger one is for washing the caravan, cleaning the cooker, the kitchen and the kitchen things. The smaller one is for washing yourself. There's a big kettle that sits on top of the burner which holds a gallon and a half – if you just leave it on top it warms in a few hours or if you want hot water quickly you just stick it on the gas cooker. And there's another bowl out there on top of the dog kennel which is for washing your hands when you come back from the woods with your shovel. There's a couple of stainless steel bowls just there next to the door – they're for washing food.

It's just practical really – living in a small space with no running water and a few people, living around animals, dogs and chickens and cats, it's easy to get worms and things like that so you have to be practical. The gypsies are more religious about things like that – but I suppose it stems from practical considerations. I suppose I'm a bit pernickety about things like that too. Like I've got my own cup which I always use and I don't like anyone else using – because it's a nice cup and because it's more hygienic.

For proper washes we can go to the local swimming baths. There's less and less of them around now unfortunately, but a good swimming baths has private baths and showers that you can use for less than a pound. The ones near here are really good. They're like a luxury hotel, better than the baths in most houses – those big old tubs with big taps that fill the bath up in about thirty seconds with steaming hot water. And you can drain it out and pour another one straightaway instead of sitting waiting for two hours while the heater gets going and warms up some more water. And the showers are like being shot-blasted – really high-pressure heads. We go there about once a week. And the kids are easy – because they're small we can wash them in here, we've got a big green plastic tub.

It's a bit awkward in here at the moment because it's too tiny when all four of us are here. The original idea was to just use this caravan as a bedroom, keep these two seats folded down permanently as our bed, so we could put the kids to bed in here and sit in the other caravan – if people are smoking, the telly's on loud or the sounds are on, it doesn't matter. But we've decided the second caravan is not completely what we want and we're trying to sell it. If we lived in it we'd never get round to doing the things that need doing to it before we sell it so we're living in here at the moment and using the other for storage. We want to get another touring caravan but a bigger gypsy-style one.

My son Laurie's in his first year of school now. His mum and Tom have bought a piece of land in Devon and put a bender up on it. They're stopping there for a while and sending him to school. He's going to stay with me during the school holidays and they can go off with their horse and cart while he's with me. That's quite an odd situation because he's shuttling between the two of us. It's quite amicable now between me and Laurie's mother. The first year or so maybe wasn't so good but it's got better over the years. It's fine now. We're both his parents and we both want to have a responsibility for our child so we make an effort. Not in any nasty way, but if we didn't have a child we probably wouldn't see each other except possibly by coincidence.

Relationships amongst travellers are different, mainly because you are living on top of each other. It puts strains on a relationship which are harder than when you live in a house. But then I don't suppose travellers' relationships break up any more than anyone else's. Very few get married. But a lot of people live as partners and do so for years, very stable. But you find out quicker if they're going to work or not.

In the last few years, especially with the kids, I've had to think about the future a bit which I never did at all when I first started ten years ago. I just lived from day to day. Now I do have to think more in the long term. I'm like most travellers really in that what I'd really like is to buy a piece of land. I wouldn't bother with a house, just put a couple of caravans on it and build some sheds, get a load of chickens and all the rest of it. Just a little spot, a little quiet smallholding where there wasn't too many people to complain and where I could just shut it all up and travel off in the summer. That's the only security I'm after really, the only thing I really want to achieve.

It's just the idea of getting old and still wondering where I'm going to go and being pushed around that doesn't appeal to me. When I'm older I'd just like to have somewhere that was mine and be able to sit there if I wanted to from one year's end to the next. It's vaguely feasible. It's just a lot of hassle. It's not just buying the land, it's then being able to live on there; getting the permission's the hard bit, getting past all the narrow-minded people who don't want trailer trash down the road.

I'd like the kids to grow up alongside other kids and choose for themselves how they want to live. Some travellers won't have their kids in schools but I think it's a good idea. I want them to be healthy and happy and do what they want. Maybe they'll rebel against us and become bank clerks. Or they might decide to do it the other way round. I spent my childhood in a house and lived like this as an adult – maybe they'll think, 'Well, I've done that as a child I think I'll try living in Birmingham for a change.' I think Laurie'll travel. He seems keen on the life. He really likes horses. And he's been to so many places – Europe, India – and he's only six and a half. He's done far more than I'd done at that age. It's too young to tell with the girls really.

Travellers always have piles of odd junk dotted around the country. They want to keep stuff but they haven't got room to take it with them at the time or it's too cluttering to their everyday life and it's not something they're actually going to use, but on the other hand it's useful and someone might want to use it or buy it one day, so you dump it in odd sheds here and there. For instance, there's only four of us living here at the moment but those sheds at the back have got about nine different people's stuff in them. They'll come and pick it up one day, odd bits and pieces as and when they need them. I've still got stuff piled around the country. At the last farm we stayed at I left some odd old-fashioned-sized tyres that fit old caravans and some windscreens out of old vehicles, stuff like that. I just took them off into the middle of the woods, put them in a bramble bush with a bit of green tarp over them and left them. I know where they are and no one else is going to do anything else with them, so if anyone ever needs it I can tell them where it is and they can go and get it. Because you make your way a lot by picking over the stuff that other people discard, you then become reluctant to discard anything yourself.

The uncertainty of not knowing how long you're staying at a place is a bit of a pain. You can't commit yourself to much if you think you might have to move again the next week. If the farmer came over and said, 'Do you fancy stopping here for the next year or two?' It would be good – I'd put some stones down where it's really muddy to make it a bit easier, it would be worth spending the money and doing the work.

This farmer's one of the nicest ones I've met really. He's young, him and his wife have got a couple of daughters who aren't that much older than our kids and he's pleasant and easy-going. He hasn't got that overbearing attitude that some of them have. Some people when you end up in this situation living on a farm and doing work, they really think they own you totally – like it's the lord of the manor up there and the serfs down here. England is a country of real contrasts, isn't it? I mean, there's a couple of hundred yards between that big house – a beautiful old place with lovely furnishings and everything, gravel drive, huge trees – and down here you've got the same sort of family unit, a couple in their late twenties with a couple of kids living in two caravans in a load of mud.

The chap I worked for before was a bit snotty like that –
he used to spend half his time off in his villa in Spain and
all that, but he was really tight and penny-pinching about
our wages. They'd spend about £20,000 on a brand-new
Mitsubishi Storm Trooper to replace one that's about a
year old at the most and the next day be quibbling about
quarter of an hour's pay. That used to get me in a frame of
mind for thinking we're well overdue for a peasants'
revolt, but it was more to do with his attitude towards it all
than the actual circumstances. With the farmer here I
don't think that way at all. I just think that's his lot in life –
he's inherited that, it's been in their family for centuries,
he probably doesn't see it as being anything great, it's
what his expectations are. My lot in life is different. He's
probably no more or less contented than I am.

I have a good quality of life really. I'm sat here – it's nice
and quiet, I've got a lovely view. Even though I've just got
a couple of small caravans to live in I don't think I'd swap
it for a four- or five-bedroom house with a view of a town.
Surroundings, your outside space, is just as important as
your inside space in my view. I've lived in Wales, right on
the top of hills where you can look round three hundred
and sixty degrees and not see anyone. That feeling of
space and privacy to me is worth a lot.

PART TWO

THE BEANFIELD
AND BEYOND

JAY

Ten years ago Jay wasn't leading the settled, domesticated life he described in the last chapter. He can't be bothered with festivals these days. When he was younger it was Stonehenge and the festival circuit that attracted him to the travelling life. He wasn't much of a hippie; he never had long hair or anything like that. He and his friends were just a bit bored. Herne Bay didn't have a lot to offer in terms of kicks: a few pubs with old men playing dominoes, or young thugs beating each other up and that was it.

In 1983 they got a bus together and headed for Stonehenge. It was going cheap so they thought 'What the hell?' That winter they wondered why they'd ever come back. They decided that next summer they'd go for it full-time. They got hold of another bus, fixed it up – a couple of beds, a burner, a range to cook on – and off they went.

At the end of the festival season they found themselves at the peace camp at Molesworth, at a time when the authorities were becoming increasingly intolerant of the so-called Peace Convoy.

In 1974 the People's Free Festival in Windsor Great Park had been brought to a violent end by hundreds of police storming the site. The public outcry that followed made the police reluctant to repeat such large-scale operations for the next few years. But by 1984 the size and frequency of the festivals were alarming the authorities to the extent that they felt they could no longer ignore them. That year 200 people were arrested at a festival at Nostell Priory, North Yorkshire. 'Operation Daybreak' in 1985 resulted in the 'Battle of the Beanfield', a watershed in the history of confrontation between police and travellers.

T here were all kinds of people at Molesworth really –
normal travellers like me, CND people, more politic-
ally-motivated green people. But a group of people came
together who stayed together for quite a while after.

We were living on the edge of the Ministry of Defence
land, quite a way from the base. There'd been a peace
camp with about a dozen people for a few years because
after Greenham it was the biggest Cruise missile base in
England. And then at the end of 1984 the Tibet Ukraine
Mountain Troupe, who used to do a lot of arts and things
at the festivals, staged a festival there because they were
moving abroad and it was their farewell bash.

People just stayed on because it was nice land there, it
was a good atmosphere. It grew really rapidly. CND got
involved. People were sending us donations. Local peace
groups were getting together and buying caravans and
bringing them up on to the site for people to come and
stay at weekends.

They built a really big kitchen and communal space for
when people used to come and visit and for the people
who lived there. It was a huge tarpaulin structure with big
wooden doors, a big stone open fireplace, a piano and an
upstairs floor where people could sleep. There were big
parties. It was a really good site until it got evicted. On
about the 4th or 5th of February Heseltine came in with
the sappers and put a great big fence round the place. He
saw us as a threat to the security of the base.

The group stayed pretty much intact though and travelled from there to several different places that winter and
spring, moving round in one big convoy, the hippie Peace
Convoy they used to call us. We went round various
festivals and were on our way to a tree fair leading up to
Stonehenge when it was cancelled, so we ended up in
Savernake Forest, which is the place we stayed at directly
before the Beanfield.

We've always been hassled in one form or another over
the years. They've just tried different tacks with it really,
different approaches. Now they're trying to change laws –
social security and the 1968 Caravan Sites Act. At the

Beanfield the idea seemed to be to give everyone a good trashing and hope that would put them off.

The Beanfield was a big turning point for everyone, I think. They'd placed an injunction on a few named people, banning them from going within five miles of Stonehenge, and that was supposedly what it was all about, but really I think it was set up from way back; a deliberate plan to give everybody a good hiding and decommission the convoy.

We left Savernake Forest heading towards Stonehenge in a convoy, then the road we wanted to travel down was blocked. There were three tipper-lorries with their backs towards us, their big tippers up, and they'd dropped gravel across the road which meant we had to take a left turning which had obviously all been decided in advance. It was an ambush basically. They were waiting for us down this road. What they wanted to do was impound all the vehicles, take everybody into custody and 'process' all of us, as they put it – prints, photographs, the whole lot. The coppers with riot shields attacked the front vehicles of the convoy, the first ten vehicles. What they didn't bargain for was that all the vehicles following behind, seeing what was happening, all started driving through this hedge, off the road into a field.

There was a sort of stalemate confrontation for quite a few hours after that whereby people demanded to be let out and the police said, 'No, nobody's going anywhere until they're taken off and processed.' Nobody was prepared to leave on those terms.

There were minor skirmishes, people trying to pull the vehicles that had been left on the road through the hedge into the field with the rest of us. Slowly but surely as the afternoon wore on they just amassed more and more forces. More and more police gathered. But they were obviously waiting for the word. There was no negotiation with the chief constable who was there and he didn't seem to really know himself. Who really knows how far these things go up? But they were obviously waiting for some sort of order to go in and do the business.

It was about late afternoon. They'd obviously got enough people by then and had got all the coaches ready to take everyone away. They came into the field. Some people stayed where they were, in their vehicles. The policemen started breaking the windows, pulling people out and bashing people about.

Seeing all this going on a lot of people then drove down through the hedge into another field, which was the actual beanfield. Then this mad sort of 'Wacky Races' episode started and lasted quite a while with people driving around this field looking for ways out, or just not wanting to stop, and being chased by hordes of police with all the riot gear on chucking rocks. It was like the Keystone Kops. They'd get one person to stop then they'd get in those people's vehicle and chase other vehicles in them. They had a couple of helicopters up above videoing it all shouting out 'Get this one next, get that one'. And we're driving round with this mad mixture of adrenalin and fear, being too scared to keep driving round and too scared to stop.

There's a quite famous picture that was on the front cover of the newspapers of the last people who stopped, this one bus. You couldn't see the actual bus. It looked like a big stick covered in ants, all these coppers with their black hats and the shields and everything, just crawling all over this bus. There wasn't a window left. There was about eight or nine people on that bus and there must have been about two hundred coppers on it. They didn't seem to care, even about women and kids. There's the famous story of the pregnant woman who was wacked in the stomach with a truncheon.

They'd been hyped up. It came out later they'd been told there were loads of big blokes with big sticks on the vehicles when in fact it was all sorts – men, women, kids, and not violent people at all. They were mad, going round trying to ram vehicles. I was in an old army truck driving round the field. These coppers got into a bus – they'd fought off whoever's bus it was and they were chasing me round trying to ram into the back of me. I mean, there's nothing to a bus. The front end of a bus is made out of wood and fibre-glass. If they'd have succeeded in ramming us in an army truck the driver would have probably killed himself. I was half-tempted to stop and let them plough into the back if that's what they wanted.

When we eventually stopped there was this copper who was really doing his nut in. It seemed like he wanted to kill me. He was out of control. He'd been hit by somebody else I think and just wanted to get his own back and hit someone in return and I was the one who copped it. He was wild. He stood on the step-plate to stand up to get into the truck. He smashed the window with his truncheon right next to my face and I got this glass all over me and he was standing there screaming at me to turn the truck off and get down. I put it into first gear and revved it up and then took my foot off the clutch so it shot forward and threw him straight off on to his back. I did it on purpose because he was obviously going to bash me and I thought if I'm going to get off the truck I'm not doing it with him waiting to bash me with his truncheon.

When he got thrown off he went mad. He was wild. By that time the cameras had turned up and they were filming what was going on and this older copper, a sergeant, came running over to pull us apart so it wouldn't be filmed. This younger one had just lost it, he was out of control.

After it was over we were taken off, put on coaches which they'd hired especially and kept standing by, and taken to various police stations all round the country. I ended up in Portsmouth. It was weird. We were sat there with one arresting officer each, all sat on the double seats all the way along the bus.

They'd stop at a police station and ask, 'How many can you take?' 'Well we've got room for six', so six of us would get off the bus and then you'd drive another twenty miles to the next police station, drop a few more off there and so on. We were all taken to specially convened courts a few days later. The charge was unlawful assembly – one of those ancient laws from the fifteenth century or something that they haven't got round to repealing. Also, anybody who was driving a vehicle was charged with criminal damage for driving round the fields and damaging the hedges. A few people had other charges chucked at them – attempted bodily harm when they'd supposedly tried to run policemen over, things like that. But they were just holding charges to keep you in the cells.

None of it stuck in the end. It just enabled them to photograph and fingerprint everybody – they wanted to get as much information as they could. All the vehicles were taken to a big pound and you couldn't get one back out of the pound without being photographed standing next to the number plate. People started getting dressed up in stupid stuff to collect their vehicles. My mate Dave went to collect his with a schoolboy cap on and shorts and a satchel. He stood in front of his bus with all this on for the police photo album.

Mine was one of the first cases up. They put about a dozen cases through in Salisbury first as a sort of tester in front of a stipendiary magistrate or something like that. Then they were adjourned, we went back again and in the end it just sort of petered out basically.

All the cases eventually got thrown out. In fact I don't think anybody actually got convicted for anything; and at the time it was the biggest mass arrest that there'd been since ancient uprisings right back in history.

The same with when we got evicted from Molesworth. The fence they put up around Molesworth – they put up seven miles of razor-wire fencing in one night – was the biggest operation the Royal Engineers had been involved in since they bridged the Rhine. This huge operation to seal the base off just because of us.

I mean, at the time you just think it's ridiculous. You had to just think of it that way – as ridiculous, a big joke – because if you started to think about it seriously it was quite oppressive really. What are they going to do with all this film they've got? All this information? All these people watching us. Helicopters hovering around the whole time. If you thought about it too much and took it too seriously it was quite intimidating.

Eventually, after we all got out of prison, or the police cells anyway, most people just sort of drifted back to Savernake Forest in dribs and drabs. That was the last place we'd been at before, so it was the obvious place to go back to. And then it was just a process of getting the vehicles back out of the pound.

The police at this point wanted to come back into the forest to, in their words, 'finish the job off', but Lord Cardigan who owns Savernake Forest – he'd probably deny that he's on the side of the hippies – but he refused to let them on to the land. He'd actually ridden with the convoy on his motorbike that day and had seen what had happened. After he refused to let them on the land, they encircled the land trying to stop anybody else from getting on, but slowly everybody drifted back.

We left there and went on to Westbury and had a festival there. It rained and rained and rained for what seemed like two or three weeks. Again there was a big cordon of police with the helicopters and everything. They got quite het up on the solstice night, thinking everybody might leave and try and do another run on Stonehenge. They had helicopters with those huge searchlight things going round the site, army and stuff creeping around. They were dead set on us not getting anywhere near the stones at all.

All in all that was a very hectic time of my life really. Those few weeks around that time – a lot of very strange things happened. The last few days we were in the forest this nutter appeared. We were all sitting in someone's bus which had all its windows broken. This person had been running around the forest for a while screaming and shouting and behaving very strangely. We were all sitting in this bus having a cup of coffee after clearing all the glass away and sticking plastic over the windows when this bloody great ten-inch carving knife comes through the plastic of the window and there was some weird TV catchphrase, some detective shit, this person said and then this manic laughter. Then he ran off into the dark. The knife had landed literally just a couple of inches away from my neck.

That was the trouble with big sites in those days because every now and then you would get actual nutters turning up, probably people who had been released for care in the community or something and they'd just turn up at festivals and they'd be the ones left behind when everyone else had gone, still wandering around in a blanket claiming they were Jesus or whatever.

This happening after everything else – getting locked up, having the vehicles taken and everything – was just a bit much. Very traumatic. When we got the vehicles back they were in a terrible state; they'd had a right go at them in the pound. My bus had umpteen holes in the radiator where they'd stuck a screwdriver through it. In my friend's bus they'd picked up the axe that was in there and took that to the carburettor, they'd taken the tops off batteries and emptied them all over inside, emptied out money boxes, stolen anything worth stealing. Really quite atrocious. Some of these are beautiful old buses that loads of work and care had gone into, people's homes.

Looking back, you can see why they did it. At that stage the whole lawless anarchy of the Stonehenge thing was really alarming a lot of people. It was getting bigger all the time, attracting more and more people, and Thatcher was a pretty draconian person. They felt they just couldn't have people behaving like that. And the sort of numbers we had then were pretty uncontrollable. I mean, road blocks and things just didn't work very well – we'd drive through them. It was inevitable they'd want to get their own back, they'd want to clamp down.

I think the police were bored and hyped up after the miners' strike and they'd learnt a lot of things from that, a lot of tactics. And I suppose they thought they'd got away with it with the miners, people didn't seem to care, so they're going to care even less about a bunch of hippies. The Conservatives are the party of law and order and we were an annoying thorn in their side, a whole troop of crazy people going out and rejecting everything they believe in and encouraging others to join them. It was the yuppie era. That's what was being rammed down people's throats – that's what you were meant to be and we were the total opposite of that.

It worked, though. Last year was the first time since then that you had big convoys going to the festivals. After the Beanfield and stuff people went off in smaller groups, doing their own thing really. It wasn't that great mass movement again. Every time we moved after that it was shedding more people all the time.

I went off to Kent then to see the woman I was seeing at the time and we went from there down to Cornwall.

With all these things on top of each other I was on the verge of a nervous breakdown. It was a very strange time. I just wanted a quiet time after that so we went off on our own, quite enjoying the anonymity of it, a bit of peace and quiet.

FLOYD

'Floyd used to be a hippie,' mocks his girlfriend Chip. 'He had a headband and flares and that. You did! I've seen you in them old photographs.'

'I was a big hairy biker,' protests Floyd indignantly. 'Only slightly flared.' These days, though, Floyd is more of a rave-head. He wears a KLF 'Transcentral' T-shirt, no longer as white as it used to be after one visit too many to the launderette. During the summer of 1991 he got into putting on raves with his mate Dave.

Floyd is a large, friendly man with long dark hair and a genial grin. You'd never take him for someone who's just spent six months on remand in Armley gaol for assaulting a policeman. Going to prison shook Floyd up a bit. One of the things that really depressed him was that he spent the time from May to October inside. It's winter again now, and he has the sense that somehow his summer was stolen from him.

Floyd seems to be one of those people who get into trouble easily, though usually he can wriggle out of it somehow. Like on Christmas morning when he took Chip's Mini out for a spin. He went into the blind corner under the Victorian stone railway bridge at the bottom of the valley way too fast, and, as luck would have it, one of the locals was coming the other way. Floyd skidded on the ice, smashing the other car's lights and crumpling one of Chip's wings. Fortunately the other driver went off without bothering to take any details. Later on Christmas morning Floyd had a go on a Scalextric set one of the site kids had been given for Christmas. He couldn't control that car on the corners either.

He is twenty-seven years old. 'Twenty-seven going on seventeen,' smirks Chip.

The trouble I got into last summer . . . it wouldn't have happened to anybody else anywhere else. It was because I was a traveller; 8th May 1992 was the day I got arrested. That was a Friday. I have to go back a week to explain my state of mind. We were living on a site in Hellifield, North Yorkshire. The Friday before we'd set off to go ten miles down to Shipley and put a party on there that weekend.

We got away with the party that night. Saturday night, obviously word had got out and the police had decided it wasn't going to happen. They came down and said, 'If you turn the sound system on after eleven o'clock at night, we'll come and take it off you.'

Sod that, we thought, we don't believe you. There was a band on up until half past eleven, still no police. They came off. But the moment we put a rave tune on the sound system, *whoom*, they were in there with riot vans, coming out of nowhere, and they had a helicopter overhead. They surrounded my bus. And I was just going, 'Yes, yes, whatever you want, OK.' And it sickened me to do that. I've done it a few times, seen the riot police chase on to site, kick a few people and then go back again and I've been halfway between them and my bus thinking, do I go after them or do I just stay and look after myself and my bus? After they've gone that feeling chews you up, that you didn't stand your ground and you didn't stand up for your mates, you just looked after yourself. That's what happened at this Shipley thing.

A couple of days later I was still bad-tempered, sulking. This police car came on to the site and they started asking, 'Have you seen this lad?' This one bloke from the site's going, 'What do you want?'

'Have you seen this lad?'

'What you after?'

'*Have* you seen this *lad*?'

People come on to the site and they're nice and we'll welcome them. Anybody will. We're reasonable people. But coming down shouting the odds and giving us grief . . .

I just looked out of the door and this bloke in the next door neighbour's caravan just leant over, picked up an empty coffee jar and lobbed it into the car's direction. 'Fuck off.' And so I picked up an empty milk bottle too and just lobbed it, only mine struck, it just hit the corner of the car, *whoom!* Apparently the police had come to serve a notice to get us to shut up after our rave. I thought nothing of it, just, who are these geezers coming on bloody shouting their mouth off at us?

About two o'clock that same afternoon, I'd just got back from signing on and I had forgotten all about what had happened earlier in the day. I was wandering up the track and suddenly all these riot police came on and started legging it up and down the site, all over. These were the local policemen I've seen for maybe three or four years, coming on to the site. I had been nice to them, they talked to me and had a laugh. Now they were charging at people in full riot gear and trying to intimidate us when we had women and kids everywhere. Kids were screaming their head off. All because of one milk bottle.

I had a jerrycan full of petrol. I picked it up, went up to the front of them and said, 'Fuck off, what do you want? I'm not scared of you.'

And one of them started running towards me. I flicked the can at him. 'Fuck off.' He reared back, took a look and then dived at me. He was a big fucker, like.

I was just off my head really, chucking that petrol about. And I had a Zippo lighter in my other hand. As soon as it became obvious he wasn't going to back down, he was just coming at me, I just thought, 'Oh, shit!' threw the can down and legged it. I realised I wasn't going to get away with it, because there were riot police everywhere arresting people, so I threw my hands in the air and they arrested me.

At first I didn't take it seriously, what I'd done. I knew these coppers, and I was just giving it a bit of bravado. I don't know what was going through my head. As soon as I went in I thought, 'Oh they're just going to keep me a bit. This is just a joke, is this.' Because I know what coppers are like. But they went, 'You're kidding, mate. There's four years on this.'

I got more and more depressed as time went on. I was devastated. It was the low point in my life. I was thinking all the things that had led me to do it. A lot of it was my beliefs, but a lot of it was having my buttons pushed from outside. They shouldn't have been able to do that to me, to come on to site in riot gear, deliberately. They didn't have to do that. They have never come on like that before. Before it's always just been a couple of them coming on in a car and saying what they want to say. But they came on that day and I wanted them to know that I wasn't intimidated by the police. They don't scare me.

While I was in containers, in custody, immediately after they arrested me, I kept meeting all these other coppers coming in. They were saying that what they'd been told is that it had taken 1,000 officers and a helicopter to move us off the Shipley site. So apparently they were expecting a war at Hellifield before they even got there. That was the sort of tension I saw in the policemen coming at me.

I was put into Armley, in Leeds, on remand. First time I was in a cell in Armley, it was horrific. I couldn't believe it. Hardly anybody came to see me. Three days after I was put away everybody on the site decided to go down south for the festival season, so the only person who came to visit me was Chip.

I wasn't used to that sort of life. I wasn't used to having to spend all my time with people like that in prison. It was like being an alien. The prisoners had a laugh. 'Oh, hear your lot is rioting again.' It was quite amusing.

This bloke Woody came to visit me. He's six foot tall, he wears a dress and a top hat and he takes pride in his grubbiness – he looks black, like the fuckin' chimney sweep off Mary Poppins. I got so much ribbing after that it was unbelievable.

The screws were all right. After a few months I got to know them. They'd have a laugh. Another mate of mine got put away with us while I was there and we got put in the same cell. Another traveller got arrested too, he was in the same place and they were accusing us of trying to set up site on B wing. There were five of us off sites in there this year.

I've been travelling about four years now. I started in about '87. I had been to a festival at Nostell Priory in Leeds in about 1984 and a lot of travelling people had been there and they really impressed me with how together they were. It stuck in my mind how much they all seemed to be playing as one, so to speak. The vehicles at Nostell Priory were beautiful, well painted up, lovely vehicles. The people were really friendly and nice. There wasn't an element of Special Brew – well there *was*, but it didn't show through. The people were fairly quiet. Well, that's a lie too. They were noisy, loads of fun, but it was a right good spirit.

At the time I was just getting into the drug culture, and that was a big draw, just wandering round the festival site and not being paranoid about smoking a bit of ganga. Generally it was all a lot nicer and freer than anything I'd ever experienced before. It's just the general oppression of living on an estate or at your parents'. You're in this bubble and everyone's looking in, and your bubble's that small and that tight around you. It's like a big black cloud above your head coming down. You get on to this site and *pffff*, it's just gone, you can be what you want to be, do what you want to do. You're not paranoid any more.

When you're going home and you know they're all staying there it's hard. I can't go home from a party, me. I can't even go to sleep if there's a party. At Linton last year we were putting parties on over Christmas, all the days and every night in this shed, and I was forcing myself to stay awake. I was wandering round with my eyes sagging. 'You coming out tonight, there's another party?' 'Oh yeah, all right.' So going home from festivals was heartbreaking for me.

Anyway, around '87 I used to share this house down in Silsden with a load of lads and we were getting too noisy for the neighbours. I thought, 'Why don't we get a van and take our party somewhere else, 'cos they don't like us round here any more?' And so it started from there.

At first five of us set off, but a couple dropped out. We bought a Leyland Redline EA van. It was a fifteen-foot box van that we were just camping with, just throwing everything in the back of the van. We didn't know what we were doing at all. We didn't have a burner or a gas stove. We just had a Primus. We'd build a bender outside.

The first night out in this van we parked it on a beach in Wales. We'd just got into north Wales and we thought, 'Right we'll go and park on the beach and have a beach party.' The sea wall came down with a steep sandy bank and then it levelled out and went out to sea. We built a bender right on the bank so the back of the bender was against it. We actually wondered why the dogs were sleeping on top of the bender on the grass bank all night. I had a laugh saying, 'It would be funny if the sea came in during the night, wouldn't it, ha ha ha!' I'd seen people with benders, taking them down and putting them up in festivals but I wasn't going to have a go in front of them, what with them being experts. This one we built on the beach was just plastic tarps on sticks. It had a polythene floor.

When the sea came in, a mate of mine, Andrew, was laid in the doorway, and he felt around him and said, 'It's cold here, isn't it?' Pitch black in this bender, we didn't have candles or anything like that. Next thing he's saying, 'It's wet in here.' He tries to lift the door up and it wouldn't budge. 'Hey,' he said, 'I think we're under water.' And just as he said that he managed to lift it up and six inches of water flooded into the bender. Him and this other lad were out of the door like whippets and the bender door just slammed behind him with the weight of the water. There must have been about eight inches by now and I was bashing my head against this sandy wall in the pitch black, spinning round in the dark, screaming. The dogs were a lot smarter than us. They had it sussed.

I've had some horrific bender experiences. They reckon once you've lived in a vehicle you can never build a bender again properly, but I could never build one properly in the first place. The first few attempts at being a traveller were a real calamity.

I went to a festival at Ribblehead. 'Right. This is where I'm staying. I'm not going home from here. All these lads here are great. I'll just throw me tarp in with theirs.' I made this stove out of a milk churn. Well, nobody said anything. I lit it. The fucking thing melted in the middle and it was dropping molten metal and cinders over us. I grabbed the handle of the milk churn and just chucked it out of the door. I had my hands in a bucket of water for three hours before they could do anything. They took me from Ribblehead to Airedale Hospital in an ambulance which is about thirty or forty miles, and they had to keep stopping at pubs to get ice for the water I had my hands in because I was fuckin' screaming my head off. It took most of the skin off my fingers and I ended up in Airedale Hospital with plastic bags on my hands for two weeks. So that was the second attempt to go out in a vehicle. But you learn. You learn.

At first it was really uphill and hard work getting vehicles because we didn't know any people. I was thinking, if I wanted to buy a bus I'd be looking at grands rather than hundreds. And then after a while I realised that it's not like that at all, you can get vehicles really cheap.

After the Leyland I had a white ambulance; it's down on the lower site now, my friend Ashley's got it. Then I sold that for £1,100 and I bought the coach next door. I was living with another lass then, called Sarah, and we had a kid. That's what we got that bus next door for, to live on that. That lasted about a year. Then she left me and I had a big bus and it was costing me loads of money and I was frightened to death. I was just on the giro and I thought if any part of it breaks down it's going to cost me at least a hundred quid. I was living in this great big forty-five-seater, thirty-two-foot-long coach, like a football pitch in there, just me trying to keep warm. So I bought this for £400 just at the beginning of this year which is a steal really. It's going to be about £150 to insure, cheap because it's got an agricultural engine. I'll give it the test, it'll pass easily enough. With buses there's not really much that can go wrong. The major selling feature is what it's like inside. It's nice woodwork, nice kitchen units, it's got a DMC engine, so it's going to be a winner. The bodywork's a bit rough on the outside, but only needs a little paint job and a little aluminium.

I got it in May 1992, then I went to gaol about three weeks after that. I've been out about two months now.

I was in remand for six months. The barrister said, 'Well, if they don't drop the charges, we're looking at several years.' I've never been as low in my life.

When it came to the court case the defence brought up that I'd already been chased off this one site and now the same was happening again. Plus the fact that they were in riot gear was unnecessary. Only one bottle had struck this car.

I had done six months on remand and when it came to the trial, they said in view of the six months I had already served, that they wouldn't give me a further custodial sentence. They gave me forty hours' community service painting roofs and moving furniture. When I heard that I was so relieved, because the charges I'd got were serious. GBH with intent. That's one step below attempted murder, I think. Plus ABH, which was petrol in the eye of this policeman – although I've got photographs of them that day and they all had visors on, so that's bullshit. Plus two threats to kill and affray. They stuck me on some really heavy charges to keep me on remand all summer, because it was only bravado. They know. I mean the copper who was covered in petrol, he chased me and caught me, jumped on me. And I had a lighter in my hand. I mean, he wasn't scared, was he? He could have stepped back and let another officer do that.

When I first came out of gaol I was more used to gaol life, having a shower every morning. After six months of showers I was bleached white. Chip used to come and visit me in prison and I'd go, 'Chip, you've got dirty nails.' I came out and any mess on me looked like soot on a wedding dress. 'Ooh, I've got to go and wash my hands!' I was putting plastic bags on my hands to get the coal. Chip would go, 'Give it here, Floyd,' and grab it with her hands. It took me a good three weeks to get back into it, to get back my tinker tan. You spend a lot of time opening stove doors that burn the skin on the edge of your fingers and they start to get crusty and mucky and it gets engrained. You have to soak it to get it out.

What you learn by being a traveller is you know you can cope. You know how far your limits go. Your limits are stretched more than when you're in a house, and you learn what you can cope with. Like some people say, 'I couldn't cope with going to gaol.' But when you go there, you cope with it. You learn to know what you can cope with and you grow.

I really like it round here, in the dales. I love it. It's not much. There's a golf course up that way and there's a gravel pit all round us, just go down there and you're down to some proper trees, not this pine stuff, none of these plantations. And the moorland.

My mum was against what I was doing at first, when I was sixteen, seventeen. By the time I was twenty, as long as I wasn't getting into trouble with the police, she was happy. My parents are fairly old, me father's sixty-seven and me mother was something like sixty-three. She was coming round to it because she had worked all her life and what's it done for her? Because she was bringing up the kids and working as a nurse. For the last eight years of her life she was ill. Could hardly do anything. So I think she came round to the idea that I was getting some life now, making it happen instead of waiting for it. Pie in the sky when you die, like. She died in 1991 of leukaemia or something. And here's me, at least I'm doing something now, rather than hoping that I can do it later.

Prison has never entered into my life before this year, but this summer I've had five mates inside. I don't know what it's going to be like in the future. It's got to get better. I could stand the politics if it wasn't for the weather and I could stand the weather if it wasn't for the politics. I've either got to get out of this country or become rich and buy a little land.

We're refugees seeking shelter. That's how I see myself, as a refugee.

SPIDER

Spider didn't have such a great Christmas: six convictions in ten days. His crime? Running Circus Normal, one of the biggest sound systems on the festival circuit.

He doesn't come across as much of a ringleader – tatty clothes, the stub of a ginger mohican and a modest, unassuming manner. But that's what he reckons the police have him down as, as if the whole traveller business was his fault. 'They can't imagine anything without a structure of leaders and a hierarchy. Travellers don't have leaders but because Circus Normal is so conspicuous they think I am one.' You wouldn't mark him down as much of a businessman either. But Circus Normal is a very successful operation. He thinks he might sell it one day, maybe make a bit of money. When he 'throws a party' – the term he uses for staging a rave – he claims he can get two thousand people there at two hours' notice.

He boasts about the New Year's Eve before last when they squatted the Roundhouse in North London and drew a crowd of fifteen thousand. Camden High Street was blocked solid twice. The crowning glory was that they were squatting on Metropolitan Police land at the time.

Spider doesn't like the police.

I remember one of the early Stonehenges back in the seventies when we just had a small PA and a generator that wasn't powerful enough to run both the band and the lights at the same time. We had the local Amesbury police shining the lights of their police cars on to the stage to light it for us.

Now, because of the work we've put in over the years, we've got a good PA, a quality sound system, good lorries, better light shows. We should by rights be having a better time of it, but all we get is oppression.

It seems the Old Bill has got it in for us – violence, impoundments, petty harassment – they're determined to stamp us out. The seed we planted five years ago is not being allowed to flower. They see us as dangerous, subversive, when all we do at the end of the day is entertain people.

I started Circus Normal five years ago just after Bill Normal died. He used to live around the festivals and I suppose he was the closest thing we had to a tribal elder. He was a Piccadilly busker for twenty-five years before he met us so he was a bit wide. He was a very talented geezer – he was a musician, he wrote books, he wrote plays for the BBC and ITV. He died from stomach cancer when he was fifty-two, very frustrated because there was loads he hadn't done. So I named the circus after him, hoping that if we got anything done his energy and example would have achieved something and if he was looking down on us he'd think 'Yeah, that's good'. Because I loved him, he was a great man.

The point of Circus Normal was to provide an environment for creativity, whatever form it takes. We'd provide generators, electricity, sound equipment, a roof, so anyone who wants to do anything can do it: bands, circus performers, jugglers, clowns, tightrope walkers, anything. We do raves now as well which is why we get in all this trouble. There's people I know doing five-year gaol sentences for putting on a dance. I think there's something seriously wrong with that on a human rights level. It's lunacy. I wish they'd just see us as a respectable profession in an old tradition, which is what we are. Times change and things take on a different shape and form but what we're doing, tribal festivals, have been happening for centuries. One of the most respectable things is ballroom dancing, that's Mr and Mrs Normal isn't it? Why should contemporary dance – which is what a rave is – be treated like it's something the devil's spawned?

Circus Normal has been built up from one lorry to what we have today with a lot of hard work, a lot of energy and a lot of cheek. I haven't signed on in thirteen years. I've always made myself a living. That should earn me a certain amount of respect. Instead I'm treated like a dangerous criminal.

At the moment practically all our equipment has been impounded for various petty reasons. They've got three lorries, all my trailers and generators, about £50,000-worth of PA which we've only just got back after six months. Would they do that to a haulage firm? The PA was taken off the road because one filament in a tail-light bulb wasn't working and one filament in a headlamp wasn't working. For two bulb filaments they've had our equipment for six months. That's a dozen families' livelihoods. And there's not been a single criminal charge, not even a traffic ticket.

I was thirty-five miles away from Castlemorton at the time and they said I was going to an illegal festival. I was on my way to Talley Valley in fact, but it happens to be on the same road, the A40, so they just presumed I was going there and were determined to impound me. It meant I couldn't run the circus for the rest of the summer. I'm suing them for £70,000 loss of earnings. It sounds a lot of money but you're talking a crew of between a dozen and thirty people and all the rest of the expenses – I spend thousands on diesel alone in the summer.

I've had it so hard off the Old Bill over the years that I don't even hate them any more – I feel sorry for them. They're seriously sick people and I pity them. It takes some treatment before you start feeling like that about them. But I've been hospitalised by the police before. Last time I was locked up it took four and a half months before anyone could find me to visit me – they hid me away till the marks had gone.

I was in gaol on a drugs possession charge and I'd escaped halfway through the sentence. What pissed them off was instead of being in hiding on the run I'd been driving the lead vehicle on the convoy for four years. One thing they don't like is spirit. They gave me a god-awful kicking. I had about thirty blue and purple truncheon weals from my head to my ankles. I had blood pouring out of my arse from internal bleeding. I had broken ribs and had to be assisted walking for a week. I was a fucking mess. They put me on what's known as the ghost train, moving me around all the time. I was at nine prisons in two and a half months so by the time anyone sent me a letter or found out where I was, I'd moved on. What can you do?

When harassing us doesn't work they go for the kids, try and take them off us. They have this idea we don't look after them properly. Unbelievable. I'm an anarchist and anarchy in my book means communal responsibility. Anybody below responsible age is the communal responsibility of anyone above responsible age. I've no less love for other kids than I have for my own. They all need feeding, they all need our guidance. Travellers' kids shine. It's funny to say there's horrible kids but there are. You see a lot of straight kids and they're horrible brats. Because of the way we live on site our kids are subject to a wider range of heads, of older minds, and that's healthy. If there's kids on sites that are a problem it's usually because they've not been here very long. They've been on a council estate or in care or something and they just do what they want, no respect for anybody.

I remember one woman who came to live behind me on a site, a single parent with a daughter and a son about eleven, twelve. They'd only been on sites for about a year and he was a fucking brat. One day I heard him screaming at her, 'You fucking cow, I hate you', all this really horrible abuse. The woman was obviously really upset, she was in tears, so I went over to him, grabbed him by the throat and said, 'Listen, sunshine, if I ever hear you talking to your mother like that again I'll wash your mouth out with soap.'

A few days later he's at it again: 'You fucking bitch, you fucking slag.' I grabbed the soap, lathered it up, flew across and pinned him down on the ground. Tears of rage. He's screaming at me, calling me a bully, all that.

A few months later we had him apprenticed to Andy, our top diesel man. Andy's on his back under the lorries doing what he does best. The lad's passing him spanners, learning about the lorries, getting really into it. Now, six or seven years later, he's fucking sound, a worthwhile little bloke.

You see, the sites are the last bus stop. If you don't get on here you don't get on anywhere. There's some that don't. Modern society creates some seriously fucked-up people – its values are twisted and perverse. And their idea of how our kids should be cared for is to be taken away from us and put in some fucking home. They call that care.

That's not about the kids, it's about us. It's a way of getting at us. They want us in gaols and they know that if they take the kids away we'll fight them and if we fight them they can gaol us. That's exactly what they did at Stoney Cross the year after the Beanfield. Fighting us hadn't stopped us so they tried two different tacks – impounding the vehicles on small technicalities and taking away the kids. They'd obviously planned it carefully over a long period. They had care orders for forty-seven named kids and they planned a dawn raid. Luckily we were forewarned.

I was lying in my bender one night when this druid comes up on a Norton Commando and says, 'Hello, I'm a member of the secular order of druids,' and tells us this story about how he'd been to a tea party that afternoon in Salisbury. Prince Charles was there and so was John Duke, who at that time was Chief Constable of Hampshire. All the time I'm thinking, Yeah, right, this sounds like a wind-up – you do get a few strangers on sites, the odd mad person turns up, people who've taken drugs start saying weird things – but I listened to him anyway. He said at this tea party he'd overheard Prince Charles talking to John Duke. At the time we was in the news a lot, the big topic of the day, so Prince Charles, trying to think of something to talk about with this John Duke, says, 'What about these hippie chappies, then?' and John Duke said, 'Well, your greatness,' – or whatever it is you call Prince Charles – 'don't worry about it, it's all in hand. In fact at four o'clock tomorrow morning the problem will be over. Sorted.'

It was about midnight when this druid told us this and as I say I wasn't sure whether to believe him. Twenty minutes later this little woman in a little car arrives on her own. I mean it's the middle of the night, the middle of the New Forest, a big travellers' site. For a straight woman to come on like that takes a bit of courage. We don't really realise what a picture we look like from the outside but I imagine it's quite intimidating – we're not like that but I can see that that's how it looks. So, for her to come on like that was quite a big deal. She says, 'Look, I work for Hampshire social services, my conscience won't let me live with this. You've got to get your kids away because they're coming on at four o'clock. The police have got care orders for forty-seven kids.' As soon as she said four o'clock, that was it. I knew the druid must have been telling the truth. It was too much of a coincidence.

We got all the kids up and put them all in this big bus and drove straight down to Glastonbury. I went to see Michael Eavis who runs the festival there, explained what had happened, and he let us park up in this field. So all the kids spent the night there in that bus. It was a very emotional night in many ways. The way those people had come to warn us was gratifying, uplifting, but the thought of what lengths the authorities would go to to drive us down was frightening.

ZED

The notice taped up near their bus reads:

In the Skipton County Court
No Of Matter: 9201672
Between North Yorkshire CC
And Persons Unknown
To [named respondent and] every other person in occupation of 2
parcels of land at Brackenly Lane, Embsay . . .

Zed, a bearded, long-faced man in his mid-thirties, has seen
scores of these in his years as a traveller. It requires representa-
tives of the residents on the Embsay site to appear in court in
Bradford on 21 December (with unintended irony, an appropri-
ately 'new age' date – the winter solstice).

Zed, Chris and their kids have been on this site a while now, so
it was bound to happen some time. The worst thing that could
happen is they start evicting right away. They've just had a new
baby, Tom. The last thing they want to do is go traipsing around
the countryside looking for a new site at this time of year. There
are no longer many sites left they can pull up on around here.

But then it's four days before Christmas. It won't look good in
the local papers, evicting travellers in the middle of the season
of goodwill. People generally get sentimental about travellers
around that time, bringing food and clothes for the kids.

Either way, Zed is going to be standing up there in that court
on behalf of the rest of the site, listening to whatever they come up
with this time and asking for an adjournment, for a little more
time . . .

W hen I was first travelling you could pull on to the
       sides of old roads, you could pull up on to drovers'
lanes, and farmers even used to invite you on to the fields
for a party. Back then you could pull on most places and
get no hassle, but now because of the press and the
government, everybody knows who we are. So within
five minutes of turning up on a bit of land you've found,
you're either going to get the police turning up or you're
going to get an irate farmer. It's usually the irate farmer
who starts threatening all sorts. With all his acres of land
he won't give you thirty-six feet. And then it gets really
silly. The last two times on farmers' land we've been
sprayed with cowshit from muck-spreaders.

We'd rather *not* park on anybody's private land. We'd
rather park on completely unused land or council land.
The second time we got muck sprayed we were at the end
of a lane which was highway land and the farmer did it on
there. It wasn't even his land. All the farmers see is that
you're trespassing and they don't want you there. They
don't care who you are or anything like that.

This layby we're on now is unowned land. The council
say it's theirs, but no one owns it. There are no deeds for
it; it's just land they started using. But because the council
dumps grit here, the council have applied for the deeds.
So we're going off to court and fighting that. We're going
and asking for an adjournment, saying we've got as much
right to be on this land as they have, but the court will
probably end up granting the council deeds in the end.

That's what happens. We were up in Markhouse Lane
in Gargrave last summer, on a drovers' track, which is no
one's land, communal land. We were parked on one side
of it, everyone had access to fields, we weren't in the way
at all. This track led to two farmers' fields. When it came to
court, one farmer claimed that because the track was next
to his field he had a responsibility to look after half of it
and the farmer who had the other field had the responsibility for the other half. We went into court and fought
about that. We proved it was a drovers' track, so it was
common land. If you look at old documents in Skipton it'll

say that in the old days the pikey people would go and park up in Markhouse Lane in the autumn. Now 'pikey' is an old word for gypsy, and you can see where they parked, that's where we parked. But it didn't make any difference. The judge evicted us and gave the land to the farmers. So they extended their fences and now there's a lane there you can get a car or a tractor up but you can't park anywhere.

We're in court in four days, on Monday. The council want us off. I know that as soon as I get evicted off here I've got a fight on my hands to take my home somewhere, and I don't want a fight. I don't want to fight anyone, but people seem to want to fight us. I don't believe in land ownership, because land ownership creates poverty. I was born into this world to survive and I'm damned if I'm going to do as I'm told.

I started in the seventies. I spent six to eight months working at a mill after I left school for £25 a week which wasn't bad, but I got really bored. One night I sat in a pub with all my mates and they were all really bored too. Someone said, 'Let's all go to Israel.' Well, you can go to a kibbutz over there and work and have a holiday, and all you need is about £300 and you can go. So that's what we did.

Five of us went. Out of the five, two are still in the town in Yorkshire where I come from, one's a Labour candidate in London and acts really *strange*, the other can't handle anything, lives with the teepee people in the south of France and takes drugs all the time. And then there's me. I'm living on the road. So two out of five of us . . .

I've never owned a home or rented a flat since I left school. After Israel I was hitching or I had cars. I was travelling around Europe. I'm thirty-four now, that was in the mid-seventies. It was easy back then. I could go abroad, come back after six months, get a job for a bit, get a tax rebate and go abroad again. I suppose you can do that still to a certain extent but you can't walk into a job like you used to. It was the festivals in the summer I used to come back for. For about five or six years I used to spend the winter in Amsterdam and then come here for the festivals. It all stems from the festivals.

The festivals were all free then, before Michael Eavis, the farmer who puts on Glastonbury, sold out and started charging. Any commercial industries run by outsiders like hot-dog machine vendors were turned off. You see, the thing about festivals is that there's no big breadhead making a butty. It's just us. I've made enough money doing food stalls, breakfasts, tarot, jewellery, all sorts of things at Stonehenge. Mate of my friend's parked on a beach for a winter with a buffer and buffed all these pebbles up, wrote 'I got stoned at Glastonbury' on them and varnished them. It cost him £60 and he sold them for a quid each. A lot of people laughed at him but he made thousands. He made a lot of money on something out of nothing.

But Stonehenge was always the main festival. I remember 1983, that was the year there was no dope on the site. Some dope come and the police pinched it. I've never seen so many people get off their arses and go over to this police vehicle. They just kept rocking it and rocking it. First the bag with all the hash in it come out and they thought we'd stop after that but we kept going until they'd thrown the people they'd arrested out as well. Then we turned it upside down.

I don't go to festivals any more because it's just rave music all the time, you can't hear anything else. It's changed a lot. The festival scene is all still happening but you've got this constant rave music going on. The last festival I went to, I didn't need drugs to stay awake all night. It was the music! You got bounced out of bed at night. Our son Rory used to crawl into bed with us because he just couldn't get to sleep. This constant battery all the time.

There's different people at festivals now like brew crews. Brew crews are a problem for society. They're what society's pumping out. They're not our fault. They've come out of the cities and have carried on living the way that they did in the squats. They've brought the problem out on to the road. And they've brought drugs out on to the road.

Years ago, if someone started selling heroin on a site, they used to get kicked off. I've took many people off site for selling heavy drugs. I smoke hash myself, and I don't mind that, but getting yourself addicted to something is something else. If you want to take it yourself it's up to you, but you can't go forcing it on other people.

I know sites in the south of England on the outskirts of Bristol where they all just sit there and hang out while someone's running into London to get a bag. They're all into heavy drugs down there. They're only living in trailers and things like that because they can't get anything else together. They don't see the environment outside. I've seen lots of trouble from heroin. It's not getting any better, and it's not any better in the system either. No matter how much they say they've got the heroin problem under control, the simple fact is it isn't, because the government are sponsoring it to keep the inner cities quiet. The whole system is in pieces. People in houses can't see it.

You've got those that like us and those that don't. You get those guys who'll drive past in their cars as fast as they can going, 'Fuckin' hippie dirty bastards.' You get local kids, vigilantes. I've got into fights in pubs with vigilantes, but never had any vehicles wrecked. I've been lucky. They think they have to have a fight with you because you're different to them. It's paranoia. They're straight and we're doing something different so they have a go at us. We had a whole pub attack us once, that was in a little place called Shepshed outside of Loughborough. Just went in and they started calling us names. Two people got up and went straightaway. I decided I'd had enough and I was getting up to go and this big yobbo started giving grief to the woman I was with then who's the mother of my eldest, Joe. So Joe's mum hit him on the head with a beer pot.

And that was it! The pub from over the road came over to have a go at us as well. We managed to take the toilet and barricade ourselves in and the landlord let us through into the bar, because you could get into the bar from the toilet, and then out the back and he locked the front door so they couldn't get out the front. In the end the vigilantes smashed up a mate's truck.

Funny thing was the next village along had all these bikers who didn't like all these geezers who'd set on us, so instead of us lot having to go and sort them out, which would have caused loads of trouble, all the bikers came over and sorted them out. Then they came up to our site and we had a big party. Halloween it was. And everything was sound after that.

It's not just the lads, either. We pulled on this place at Hellifield, which is about ten miles away, and the next minute all this wood and trees were put in the way of the gate, blocking it. At first I thought it was the farmer, so I cleared it all and opened the gate, and by the time I'd got back they'd done it again. But this time I saw who was doing it just as I rounded the corner, before they ran off. It was kids, ten- to fourteen-year-old kids. They hear the parents talking about us in bad terms and automatically they assume they can do things like that.

'Our patch,' they call it. 'Our patch.'

I don't really know what's going to happen now. I know myself that they can't really bring these laws in, like the reform of the '68 Act. We won't disappear, no matter what laws they invent. If they brought out a law tomorrow saying I was illegal, I'd still be sat here in my bus. And if someone comes and says you can't park here any more, well I'd just have to park in laybys overnight. We'd still be here. You'll just get thousands of travellers stopping in laybys all the time.

We're trying to get it together to go abroad, and take this bus over into Europe, but Tom being born has stopped our plans. He just happened. Now we've got two kids, three with Joe. Joe's going back to his mother who's a traveller too, back to the Gower in south Wales, back to a bender life, and hopefully I can get the bus abroad for a while. We can go travelling about before the young ones get to school age.

I want to travel all the way down south . . . Just carry on down south and see where we end up.

PART THREE

A THINKER,
A VISIONARY, A SEEKER

DECKER JOHN

For the residents of the Embsay site in North Yorkshire, December 1992 started with the Paul McCartney fiasco. It began when a woman called Beverly came knocking on their bus doors asking if they wanted to be in a pop video. She'd give them each £25 a day to be in it. 'Who is it?' they asked. 'Paul McCartney. It's for a song of his called "Hope Of Deliverance".'

The travellers considered the proposition. Decker John thought the idea of using travellers as a backdrop for a video was one of the most condescending things he'd ever heard; besides, he was more of a John Lennon man himself and £25 each was hardly a fortune. But then if everyone got the money, it would leave the site with a fair bit of cash. Chen, the poacher from the caravan next door thought it might be a laugh to meet a pop star. 'Get your hash out, McCartney,' he'd tell him.

So they agreed to do it. The day before the shoot the film company wanted all the big vehicles to be driven up to the location, high above Pickering on Goathland moor. The next day, at seven in the morning, everyone else got driven up there in a Transit.

Predictably, the shoot was a disaster. For a start, it poured down all day and the wind howled over the top of the moor. The brakes on Zed's bus faded as it was going down a hill and it smashed into another vehicle and out came the windscreen. For the rest of the day he had to drive around without any glass in front of him, while Chris, eight and a half months pregnant, sat in the back. If Chen was a little disappointed to find Paul McCartney wasn't going to be there because he was in New York, he was completely outraged to find that they'd laid on a Linda-style vegetarian buffet for the travellers. 'If I'd known,' he complained, 'I'd have brought me ferret and gone and got a couple of rabbits.'

Finally, much to the travellers' bemusement, a bloke called Jeremy who seemed to be in charge asked them to walk alongside the buses holding lighted torches. The wind and the rain kept putting the torches out. It was freezing. Jeremy finally blew it as the shoot dragged on towards dusk and the travellers started asking for more money. He lost his temper and started shouting and swearing at them, so they started shouting and swearing back. The whole day was a washout. Two days and hardly a second of film worth using.

'I had a lot of fun, me,' said Decker John afterwards. The day had confirmed his belief that it wasn't him that was eccentric wanting to live in a bus, it was the rest of the world that was a bit funny in the head: 'I thought they were very silly.'

Three weeks later the Sun got hold of a story about Paul McCartney using new age travellers as extras for the video and printed it under the headline: 'Fury As New Age Scroungers Get £20,000 Off Mac.'

John's double-decker looms above all the other trailers, cars and buses parked up on the layby. The concertina doors are heavy to pull back, and the lower floor is full of bits of engine and tat. At the top of the stairs there's a trap-door you have to push up.

Crouched by the burner, halfway down the bus, are John and his daughter Claire. On the other side of the partition are the bedrooms John has put in. There's a record player and a battered stack of old LPs. At the front of one pile there's one by Melanie, at the front of the other, one by the Grateful Dead. Pinned up on the walls are Claire's moody poster paint landscapes, made even moodier by the guttering candlelight. John's two big dogs jostle for space in front of the fire, but they're never there for long before John slaps them to get them out of the way of the heat.

For years, John travelled with his partner and their eight children. In the end the local social services department encouraged them to move into a house in Skipton, but it turned out that the house wasn't big enough for ten people. Now seven children live with their mother in Skipton, while John and one daughter live on a large green double-decker bus in a layby outside the site.

It's blatant. The sheep have it all. We have nothing. Look out of the window. Every field you look at has got sheep in it. Down here around Skipton it's not so bad, at least down here they earn money selling sheep. But further north you get *token* sheep, you get it down to as little as three sheep per field. They're not actually earning their keep, they just sit in the field and say, 'I am a sheep. This is a sheep field, therefore nothing else is allowed in here.' You can't walk your dog there, you can't even go in a sheep field. It's just so obvious to me how much land the sheep have, so many acres per square sheep, and how little land we have.

But it shouldn't be the be-all and end-all.

We've lived in this area about three years and we've had twenty-two different evictions. You keep trying to find places where you won't upset no one. Since we've had this bus we've run into this bunch of hippies that are surrounding us now. They've got all of us on a gravel tip on the side of a road, and it's dangerous, not really fit for human habitation, but there's nowhere else to go. The sheep have all the green fields and we haven't got nowhere. All that's left is sheep land.

I come from a farm cottage on a hill on the Lancashire–Yorkshire border, so whichever side of the hill you went down, they thought you came from t'other side, because nobody came from the middle, like. So I've always felt a bit alienated in England. This is how I chose to live my alienation.

Travellers aren't a totality, like. It depends which travellers you start looking for. There are people out there who are typical travellers, but I'm not one. I've never been off the island, me. Not once. Went to the Isle of Man once, when me mam was feeling rich, and a seagull shat on her hat. She didn't like it. It were a new hat, special. That's a true story that.

My father were a coalminer. They've shut those pits down now. He was an old chap when I was born, seventy-four, died when I was ten years old. Could have done with him being around a couple more years. When he was a boy my father used to catch sparrows and take them home under his hat for tea. They were hungry days. Folk used to live on their own croft on their hill doing what they did. But then they brought this compulsory schooling in. It's the same thing they did when they took India – put the schools in first and the next generation will be subservient. So you're teaching them to want all the things you've got, and then they have to work for you, don't they? That's what they've done to the English, and most of the English don't know it because they'd have to go back a generation or two to bloody see it, like.

I've got a brother. Only one. He's a funny bugger, a Catholic. He went to fight for the British Army in Northern Ireland. They don't come any stranger than that . . . I didn't want to do any of that. Pass, mate.

When I was about eight year old I remember I found a very big, strange-shaped piece of copper by the road. It was a two-foot tall cone with a tube off it that would be about two-foot long that went down to a little bowl thing. Nowadays I could tell you that it was a copper still, but I didn't know what it was then, of course. So I took it home and my mam said, you'll have to take that to the police. So we took it to police and they looked at it and they said, 'It fell off the top of a circus wagon, that.' And I think that ever since then I've wanted to know what sort of circus wagon you had to have to have one of those on top. I joke that I've been looking for a wagon like that ever since.

I used to be a carpenter and joiner. I started off in a workshop, but there wasn't much of that about and there were just buildings sites to work on. I resigned from that, said I don't want any more. Wood kept getting worse every year. Every year they used to cut the trees younger and they had less time to dry. Houses aren't meant to last as long as they used to. You can get better wood out of hundred-year-old houses than you can ever buy.

I don't like cities. I go in when I have to. I know we've got to go to Bradford on Monday for the court case. There's a court order for us to appear there on 21

December. I'm not looking forward to it. I don't know if
Bradford's a city, but it's getting bloody near it.

I spent maybe a month in London. Didn't much like it.
What always puzzles me about London is why they have
double-glazing in tube trains that makes everybody look
ugly. Why? Because I'm sure them people would be a lot
more likely to lift their heads up if they didn't look ugly
when they saw themselves int' window. In London
they've got a thing about looking at their shoes. What else
can they be doing? I can never work it out.

Sky is what it's about sometimes. I was in a town once
and I only had a little cheese-shaped piece of sky out of
my window. I used to sit and wonder what happened to
the big dome of sky. When I used to live on the hill it used
to be below me, all the way round.

I don't like getting ripped off of my sky. And another
thing, it's orange in towns. You can't see out of it. They
don't have real skies in towns. I'm not keen on that
orange. Really, I don't think people should live under it. If
you look at it at night all the orange bits are theirs and all
the black bits are ours. The orange says, this is ours. This
is how much sky we can afford to light up.

I can't remember how long I've been a traveller. I've
lived in buses, I've lived under hedges and in phone
boxes, in church porches, in forests, in houses and more
houses, in people's flats. I've lived on a few fixed caravan
sites too. That wasn't a happy compromise, because it
gives somebody the power to say I don't want you here. I
don't want to be anywhere I'm not wanted. Where they
don't want me I'm quite happy not to be, but there's got to
be somewhere where they'll just leave you alone to get on
with your life for a bit.

Space. It's all right if you're rich, in't it? You can buy it.
I've spent a lot of time being poor. I'm not poor at the
minute because I've bought and sold a few buses, but I
don't have money to buy land. Not a hope in hell. And if
you buy land they won't let you do anything with it. So
it's not yours anyway. It gets more difficult all the time.

I bought two acres of moorland once above Hebden Bridge near Heptonstall by a pub called the Shooters, and we spent the winter on it. At the time it was a novel idea, buying a bit of moorland. But they cut off everything they could cut off. They threatened to cut the water off, but we didn't have any. A postman used to come past the trailer every morning to the farm at the end. He was a happy smiling postman, who would have given us the mail, but they wouldn't let him. We didn't go a lot on mail anyway. They threatened to cut the sky off too but they didn't know where the switch was.

We got right through the winter there until April, then in April we had a big snowfall one night. Eight foot of snow came down and covered our trailer. There were seven of us living in that trailer at the time. I thought, 'I've got to get these people out of here. I've got to do something about this.' And I wandered off into t'snow and I got lost trying to look for a main road that were only a couple of hundred yards away. I was sinking up to my chest in snow. I shouted, 'Help,' and this flock of water birds took off from a reservoir which was a little bit in front of us, so it's lucky I didn't carry on that way. I didn't know where I was, getting colder all the time and thinking, 'I don't like this. I wish I were back int' trailer even though it's under snow.' In the end I found a shooter's hut, full of leaves, and I had my matches and my baccy in my pocket, so I made a little fire in there and waited till the snow stopped and the daylight come. And then we moved into a council house. That very day.

Eight years ago I started living in buses. I remember the first vehicle I lived in. It was a Bedford 300, a bus, and it was pretty. I'm still looking for a prettier one, anyway. I lived in that for three years with seven children and my missus. At one time, when I started, you could drive a bus on a car licence but they play tricks with you and the games change. They've changed the rules round now. They're still doing it. It's harder to be legal now.

Then we were in trailers for a bit in Gargrave. I had one on the back of a truck and there was another down below on the ground. We'd had these big winds and one day I had just lit a fire in the burner in the trailer on the back of the truck and I went down the stairs to the other trailer while I waited for it to get warm. I can remember thinking, 'Yeah, it could do with more wood now.'

I don't know what happened, it had something to do with me opening the door, but when I opened it, the door of the trailer became the chimney. There was just a tiny hole in the front of the stove which you could look through and the flame came out of there. I saw it happen. Flame leapt out of the front of the burner, got the curtains and went whoosh. Straight at me. I was about four foot up on the back of the truck and the force threw me backwards. The whole thing happened in forty seconds. It's the only fire I ever had and it just burned everything. It took the side of the trailer off and everything blew off over this big open flat field. All my joinery tackle was buckled. My saws all went blue, and ended up without any handles on. I lost all my books, a lifetime's worth, herbal books, I Ching books, books about mechanics, scattered all over the field. There were pages from my books everywhere and bits of wadding from my caravan.

There was nothing but a pile of ashes was left on the back of this truck, and this stove. I said, well, at least I've got my stove left. And then the fire engine came. We'd already thrown enough water on this truck to make sure that nothing else will burn but this bunch of firemen come up dressed in black and yellow, like wasps. And I said, 'Please don't spray my stove.'

But they went and did it and it was still hot so it cracked. Bang. It was an alright stove.

Worst thing about it was I had just sold a really lovely truck and I'd got the cash for it. It was the first time I'd had a thousand pounds in cash and it was great. And that was tucked in above the window. We were finding bits of burned £20 notes for weeks and not able to put any two together. I never found a penny, just half a dozen bits of notes. I don't think I've got over it yet. I've got a few of my books back, and as they start to come back I feel better.

That fire I had was bad but lucky things still happen. This bus happened to me. We were just living in a tarpaulin under a tree before this, after we lost our trailer. We put two tarpaulins in a square, two of them together to make a cross, and put a very little hole in the middle of them, the size your finger goes through, and put a rope through it. We threw the rope over the branch of the tree and pulled it up, then pegged the bottom out and that was it for about four months. It was all right. It was like living in something that was alive because the tree took the wind and pulled the rope and the rope took the tarpaulin. The bottom was all pegged and fixed with stones, but the top used to move all over the place. It used to make noises.

We've been in this bus about two and a half years, us and the two dogs. I like one of them, the other one's a pain in the arse. People ask, 'Why do so many travellers have dogs?' Same reason as so many house dwellers have dogs. Dogs make a lot of noise when people are prowling about outside, and it's best to know sometimes. It might be your gen going missing or it might be your tool box. Who knows? They do your worrying for you. You can sleep.

I like buses, collecting them, mending them, crawling about under them, smelling of oil. Bus wrestling I call it. Since we landed on this layby I've bought three buses, sold two. Got one left. I just exist on the dole and see what comes along. Things fall on you from the sky.

I'd love a yard of my own, to park a couple of buses in and send them out shiny, oh yeah. That would be ideal. I can mend engines. I've much to learn about metalwork and the outsides of them, a lot to learn about that. I like the wood bits. Wood bits is good. Metal bits are a bit shaky. But I can do engines. Sometimes I get paid, sometimes I don't get paid.

This double-decker had seats in when I got it. I've been in it two years, and I'd have finished converting it if I gave it one final push. I put the rooflight in because I got fed up with not being able to stand up properly upstairs. That slowed me down a bit. When I bought the bus the idea was to live upstairs and run a café downstairs by the side of roads, not particularly for festivals, more for the tourists. But since then I've spent too long round here and my bus has got hippie written all over it, or rather 'new age traveller' as they call it now, which is a strange kind of stigma. It's not one I object to a lot, because they're all nice people. But being a hippie doesn't go down well with the council when it comes to applying for a licence to run a café.

Getting round in a double-decker is a bloody nightmare. You can suss the bridges, but it's the trees that are the enemy. I've driven round the same corner a dozen times, and one time I went round it and there was just a bit more leaf on a tree there than there was before and I pulled off a branch nine inch round. I'd been under that tree so many bloody times and nothing had happened. And I could see it through me back window heading for this fancy four-wheel drive Daihatsu or whatever they call them. But its little leaves got stuck on the rest of the tree and swung it out of the way so it landed harmlessly on to the grass. That were bloody lucky.

I'd sell the decker for that reason. If they'd let me drive from upstairs it would be all right. I could see what was coming.

If I had a thousand pounds I'd buy a Leyland Octopus and a trailer. Vehicles is where it's at. Collected wealth is what you've got in your motors. They swap and change quickly. You need money, you sell somebody a bus. They need money, they sell you it back.

The authorities don't seem to know what to do about us, but every now and again they have to make a show of force, that they've got more than we have. They'll turn up en masse for no crime at all, just to prove the point again that there's more of them than us, even though there aren't, not if we all got together. It's like Custer and the Indians, isn't it? They don't want to round us all up because if they put us all together we'd take a load of space up! And yet they don't want to leave us alone in little groups here and there either.

I think if they don't sort us out with somewhere to live pretty soon I think there will be a war goes on. If everybody gets to the point where we all decide we're going to the same place something will happen. I know that none of us want it, but we can't disappear. It's not that we don't want to. We can't.

I'm forty now and I don't know how folks should live. I don't claim to know. It's funny, because you speak and you're trying to defend a whole nation of folk in a way. If we had space we'd flourish and we don't have space. Space is what's needed. I've seen a few bits of this country, and I still think that the less people per square mile, the happier folk are.

SAM

The Dongas Tribe have fled to the hills. They'd been camped on Twyford Down just outside Winchester for eleven months, battling valiantly against the M3 extension ploughing through their beloved Dongas, the ancient tracks that cross over the Down. They'd reasoned, argued, fought, formed human chains, staged massed sit-ins, lain down in front of bulldozers, but all in vain. In November 1992 they were forced off the site and here they are a few miles away, tucked away in a little copse just outside the small town of Alresford.

If it wasn't for the communal van, a little Mini that's conked out anyway, the scene could be from any century you'd care to pick: a few teepees dotted about, smoke billowing from their chimneys, surrounding a big campfire.

The tribe's founder, Sam, is crouched on the end of her bed in her teepee, tossing small scraps of wood into the burner. It's chilly in here. There are pros and cons with a goat. On the one hand you can milk it twice a day and satisfy all your cheese and yoghurt requirements. On the other hand it can knock your chimney stack on to your canvas and burn a hole in the roof of your teepee.

It's a sparse dwelling – just a bed, a low table and a couple of up turned logs for seats – but it's homely. Hanging from the branches that form the beams of the tent there's an array of pans, jars, candles, shawls, blankets and brightly coloured garments. Dotted about the place are the fruits of the various activities that make up Sam's livelihood: the hats she crochets and sells through a shop in Wales, the pictures she paints, the jewellery she makes, the exotic musical instruments she plays and the basket weaving which she's just started learning to do.

Sam is dressed in a smock, leggings and a pair of leg-warmers, her dark hair neatly scraped back off her forehead. She's serene and self-assured. Her voice is soft but firm and bears the trace of a slight London accent. She stays crouched on the bed, feeding the fire as she talks.

The protest isn't just about the M3. It's much broader than that. It's about the way we live in the contemporary world. The way we're destroying the planet. What the Dongas Tribe is about is reclaiming the land and trying to re-establish a vital tradition, the tradition of nomadism and living on the land, living and working alongside nature as opposed to working against it, trying to conquer it and destroy it.

The people I really admire are the hunter-gatherers of millennia ago who actually lived on the land and created all the stone circles and the earthworks and barrows. They actually knew the whole cosmos really well – how it worked and how its energy functioned. That's who I'm really interested in and who I really live by – the old witches, the knowledgeable healers, who knew herb law and food law. They were like wise mothers and brothers who just knew the garden, the garden of the earth. Their knowledge goes back thousands and thousands of years. That was all trashed in the medieval years, the middle ages, by the Christian church. All the knowledge that was ever gained about how the world works was trashed. Our ancient ancestors understood the chemistry of everything, but in a more sort of – not spiritual way because that word's really abused – but more cosmically. What each mineral and plant is for, what its make-up is, what its character is and seeing it as a living thing with character like individual stones or plants or whatever and not just seeing it as dead matter to be used and abused and sold off and manufactured into something.

It's essential to re-create that, but the present system does its utmost to try and block that out and pretend that it doesn't exist, that the natural world is just a dead thing for us to consume. If they stopped trashing the earth's energy the earth would just grow and be twice as strong as she used to be. If we stopped drilling for oil and using it for petrol and turning that into gases that pollute the atmosphere, she would renew and regenerate straight-away because she always is regenerating, but the system we live by is always stopping it. The system's also trying to stop people getting in touch with the earth; that's why they're trying to stop nomadic life. To live the way we do should be simple and easy, but it's made difficult for us. For instance, we're forced into the situation that we have to use cars and roads really, it's impossible to get around otherwise. Ideally I'd like a cart and horse or even just a horse or a mule with saddle bags, but you can't travel around the landscape on the back of a horse the way it is now because there's fences and gates all over the place and farmers' shotguns. One of my ambitions is to reopen paths and make more paths. A lot of paths that are supposed to be public pathways, really ancient ones, have been allowed to grow over and have been encroached by farmers. I'd like to get that whole way of moving around accepted and feasible. We have a transport problem because everyone is travelling on the road, but if there was other ways of travelling round there'd be less. Imagine if we had little rickshaws and other little vehicles – it would be so much more exciting and less hostile and fast. Everything would slow down which would be much nicer.

I started out living in a houseboat when I was nineteen, squatting on the Thames. I moved in with a friend. When we split up I moved in with my neighbour on the river. He's still with me today. We went off and lived in France for a while, to do fruit picking. We stayed on this land that belonged to a countess, a big vineyard. She had some rooms there but the forest was just so nice, totally wild – she had wild boar and pigs and things on the land – and she didn't mind us living in the forest. We just fixed up a bender and lived in that. We met a guy who made wooden musical instruments and we ended up doing that as well because Stef and I are both musicians.

All the instruments we made were from stuff that was around in the forest. We had a friend who had a massive herd of goats, she had loads of skins and gave us the skins – these instruments have a drum thing at the front which we made out of the goatskins, the bridge is made out of a shell or a nut. We'd use gourds, a vegetable-type fruit like a pumpkin. Stef was making these guitar-type things out of one end; he'd cut it in the middle and use the rounder bit, I'd use the smaller bit. There was loads of bamboo and cane there for the bows and she had a horse – she let me snip some of its hair for the bows too.

We stayed there for over a year. It was lovely, really hot and there was so much food. There was a lot of land and a farmer rented some of the fields to grow vegetables. All you need to make a ratatouille with – peppers, tomatoes, aubergines, courgettes – were in the fields and we were allowed to just take as much as we needed. There were also big watermelons and yellow melons as well. And hundred-year-old cherry trees. In the springtime we got these big juicy black cherries, the best ones that cost about ten quid a pound in England. We had all this wonderful food for nothing.

It was idyllic for a while but I was desperate to meet more like-minded people who could speak the same language as me and understood where I was coming from with my interest in the land, especially the neolithic workings of the land, the stone circles.

The stone circles vary so much. A lot of them are marking points of cosmic events to do with the sky, to do with angles and points or maybe when a comet went by or something like that. And on a more down-to-earth level, they are a means to amplifying whatever energy you put into them. Our ancient ancestors who built these things were closer to nature and closer to their distant ancestors, handing down knowledge and stories for thousands of years. We've lost that link with our ancient past, people

can't even believe that we used to be tribal, they think
we've always been civilised Roman types.

I came back to England to find people who wanted to
understand all this a bit more. Stef and I spent a lot of time
visiting ancient places of power, neolithic workings all
over England and in Corsica as well. Lots of things came
together for me in terms of what they were about and how
music and stones have a connection. The people who
used them would have used a lot of music around the
stones because it creates incredible amounts of energy
and if you play music around a stone circle, which I've
done, you do have this aura of really powerful energy
with you and everything you do from there on becomes
really magical. And lucky. Loads of luck happens for you
because of the really positive energy that you've made.
The stones amplify whatever you put into it because
they're really powerful, they're like the computers of the
earth and the ancient world. It's quartz crystal, most of
the stone – it's no coincidence that they use quartz crystal
so much in electronics.

When me and Stef started going round visiting stone
sites and walking the ridgeways we tried to live very
differently, taking no money with us and only a small
amount of food just to see how our luck would go and
we'd just have the most incredible times. We'd meet
people. One time we got stuck in a motorway service
place and it was pissing down with rain. We didn't want
to stop our journey but the weather was so bad and we
didn't have anywhere to go. They wouldn't let us stay
inside to sleep on the floor – the people were so formal
and silly, they just kept saying it was against the rules – so
we were asking people if they could give us a lift back to
London, so we could stay somewhere. We met these
people who took us back to their place in Shepton Mallet
near Glastonbury and this guy happened to have all the
medieval instruments you could imagine. He did twelfth-
century dancing and his friend did all this beautiful
artwork for children's books. All the pictures would be
from nature – there'd be someone playing an instrument

and his clothes would be made of leaves, sewn up with grass and the instrument would be made from an acorn or something. She was a druid as well, so we got on really well. We just found lots and lots of coincidences and good things happening like that when we were visiting the stones.

It was the same with everybody meeting on Twyford Down and forming the Dongas Tribe. When I had been in France for a while it was so ideal that we wanted to get friends of ours to come over. Nobody did in the end and we just got really lonely. I really wanted to live like a tribe, with a group of people, because it's much easier and more fun. You get bored with just two people, no matter what you're doing. We were saying that when we got back to England we'd try and gather a tribe together and see what happened. We got into the idea of building roundhouses as well — round thatched-roofed huts with sides made from wattle and daub, woven hazel and cowshit basically. Or there's another way of building them where you have canvas sides which is kind of better because you can transport it. There's a guy in Teepee Valley who makes them and they're really lovely, with little windows in them and the thatched roof made of panels so you can take it apart and move it and reassemble it.

A tarot reading helped us decide to come back to England as well. Sometimes I use them just to reassure myself — they're a form of guidance because you do need some form of oracle. The reading said if we stayed in France the Devil came up. Then when it came to going back to England the Priestess came up, which is a really good card — it's the universal goddess really, the universal guide, a sound clever card. So we thought, 'Great, let's go back.' We arrived in Portsmouth and weren't sure where we wanted to go but we remembered that we'd come through Winchester on the bus when we'd been back visiting for a month and we remembered seeing St Catherine's Hill and the whole town seemed really nice so we decided to go there. Also it was cheap because it's not that far from Portsmouth. So we arrived here and we suddenly

met so many people. That day we made about five or six
solid friends immediately. We get a lot of attention, two
people walking round dressed slightly differently. People
come up and want to take your photograph, especially if
you've got an instrument. I was holding a harp and I had
quite a multi-coloured top on as well. This woman Mar-
got, who I'd met about two years before at Greenham,
came up to us. I'd been up there visiting to give them
some food and she was there. So we met her again and got
involved with her and via her we got involved in Twyford
Down and the campaign.

Things started coming together. We decided the only
way to do anything was by living on the land. Whether
we saved it or not at least we got to live on it because it's
really beautiful land. Another reason for coming back at
that time was that I really wanted to celebrate Halloween
again on Silbury Hill in Wiltshire. It's the biggest human-
made hill in the world and it's got a great story to it. It's
this enormous mound with a shape round the outside
filled with water, a lake. And the shape is like the old
goddess shape, a crap word to use because it doesn't
describe it very well. It's like a big fat pregnant woman
basically, with enormous tits and a big belly. And it hasn't
really got a head just a long extended neck. It's the most
commonly-found archaeological thing in the world, that
shape made out of clay. It's like the Priestess card in the
Tarot, it's the universal cosmic mother who does it all,
knows it all and creates all, which is what they all believed
in. The whole male God idea came round a lot later. All
over the world if you look into it, everyone believed in this
concept of the cosmic mother – it's obvious, if you look at
all nature it's the female that gives birth and creates it all.

Anyway, at Silbury Hill it's got that shape but it's flat on
the ground and full of water except for this big hill where
her stomach would be. It's all tied in with what they called
August harvest moon. The moon of August rose up over
the horizon and it came over the hill and as it came over
the reflection of the moon in the water came out where
her cunt would be so it looked like she was giving birth to

the moon. As it moved round, the light of the moon really shone in the water, especially round the area of her breasts so then it looked like she was producing milk. It was cosmic land art by our incredibly intelligent and exciting ancestors. If you look into what these things are about they're quite interesting and quite playful. People have this image of weird, sinister rituals whereas they were actually fun and playful and beautiful. It doesn't work any more because the lake isn't there, the chalk hill has grassed over and, because the earth has turned, it's slightly out of sync. But it's still a fascinating place.

The Twyford Down is really important. It was the heart of tribal culture. It was the tribal centre of old England, of old Europe really. It was a major trading centre for wool, something really really big in the world, and people from all over Europe used to come parking their boats up at Southampton, walking to Twyford Down and down into Winchester. So in terms of historical importance it's obviously a major place. You've got Stonehenge and all that on postcards but this place is much more significant. You go down to the town and there's loads of postcards of Winchester Cathedral and booklets all about Winchester and they never once show St Catherine's Hill and it's a really mega place.

People have come from all over the place because of the motorway protest and because of the good thing that was happening on the Dongas. I think it was fate that brought us here and fate that brought the members of the tribe together. We've got a main core group of the tribe now, about twenty people, and other people come and go. They've actually found something they want to get involved in. Loads of people just want to live in a traditional way and they saw that that was happening, I suppose because there was me and a few other people who knew that was what we wanted and that was the vibe we gave off. It also gave protesting a new face really. Instead of standing there with banners saying 'We protest', we actually practically stopped it by living on the land. I was planning to build a roundhouse on the down to claim the land as my own. There's a medieval law that says if you build a house or shack or something between sunrise and sundown and have a fire in the hearth by sundown and it's all made with local materials then you can claim the land. But it just never came together. Every time we tried to start it something went wrong or we couldn't get the right materials or something like that. It obviously wasn't meant to happen, but it'll happen somewhere else. I really want to get a roundhouse project started and to make it an educational thing, get some kids involved. We have a lot of plans that we want to get on with. We want to grow a lot of things and get as self-sufficient as we can.

I want to really challenge what's happening with the changes to the law in terms of travellers. Not as a rebellion thing but to say that it is a necessity to live like this, a necessity to the whole eco-system that people actually live on the land and look after it properly because that's our job on the earth. The world's been falling apart since people stopped living on the land and respecting it. The modern way of life destroys the earth. I want that to be accepted and be part of the education system. And I want to get back to the old ways a bit, people wanting travellers to come in.

I want travellers to change too, not just behave like mindless brew crew suffering under the system. It would be so good if they did get their arses into gear and started craft fairs and made festivals a bit more how they used to be. These big rock festivals tend to do a lot of damage whereas if you had lots of small acoustic folk festivals it would be a lot more interesting. And there is something new happening. Electric music is going nowhere. Rave music is just the end of it. Trashy music.

The festivals that travellers have now are horrible, hostile brew crew nightmares. I went to one last year and hated it. Then I went to an English country fair, you know with all the nice local people and pots of jam and it was so boring and dry. We should be putting a lot of effort into making exciting festivals that everyone can enjoy. What the Dongas Tribe is about isn't a case of going backwards, just living how people used to live because it seems charming when you look back on it, it's carrying on some good solid sound traditions that we've strayed from, and straying from them has been harmful. At a few meetings we've had between the Dongas Tribe and local people we've got to know through the protest, we've made the point that we should stick together and try and be a resource for each other. If we can produce crafts and that and have fairs and festivals that they could get into and enjoy, it would be a good thing.

We've made some strong links with the local community through the protest. When we came along they were knackered, this thing had been going on for twenty years. They needed us and were glad of our help. I mean, I'm knackered after a year, although that's been really intense, living on the central reservation of the road scheme.

We gave the protest a new shot of energy. Of course, now there's people getting in touch with us from other road schemes – there's about forty road schemes going through at the moment with protest groups opposing them – but we're not going to be a bloody rent-a-mob for every road protest that's going on. It's not a career.

We were actually living on the landscape; it was still a really beautiful landscape. We built a deep long trench – it was wiggly with a dragon's head at the end and crystals for its eyes and we stuck fire torches in its nose. We made barricades and decorated them really beautifully and we put little information packets on the gates.

Someone had to be on lookout the whole time really because they'd suddenly just come over with their diggers and try and trash our gateposts or the trench. We held them off for two months. One day when we didn't have many people around they managed to get past one of our main blockades and put a fence up. As soon as they'd got the fence up that meant that they could have the night lights and security caravan up there, right next to our camp. We lived next to those people for a month or

so and ended up being on quite amiable talking terms
with them. They even helped us sometimes and told us a
few things that were happening. They said to us, 'Be
really careful on the morning of your court date' – we
were going to court with Winchester College who own
that bit of land. We had a warning call, 'Arruga, arruga',
like the noise the submarines make in films, we had that
as a warning call, a sort of joke. But that was our signal.
Anyway, that call came out on the morning of the case.

It was still dark, quite early in the morning. I got up and
there was just hundreds of these blokes, big hulky blokes
in these luminous yellow jackets. We couldn't really work
out who they were or what they were doing. There was
about thirty of us on the site at the time. And loads more
people kept turning up as the word got out, everyone
who'd ever been involved, but by then it was too late.

We saw a vehicle coming over the horizon and a load of
us tried to get up and stop it from coming through, but all
the yellow jackets just linked arms around the side of it,
made a human chain to stop us from getting inside the
area. Some of us got in and just tried to get under the
wheels; our whole strategy was to get in front of the
wheels so they couldn't move the vehicles.

It just went on for hours. It was excellent. One of the
women picked up a load of mud and was wiping it on
their faces. All these guys were standing there like dum-
mies, they couldn't move their arms or they'd break the
chain, so they had to take it. Everyone started chucking
mud, like this enormous childish mud fight. Then we
started flicking their hats off. They just had to stand there
taking it, getting really, really angry. They were just
ordinary people, YTS scheme people, ex-miners, normal
security guards, just ordinary people like us really. It was
a real shame that we were put in this position where we
had to kick shit out of them as well as them kicking shit
out of us. A lot of them didn't even get told what it was
they were going to be doing – they were just hired to
guard a bit of land for a day. They didn't realise what was
going on. We were so hard for them, we really were. I feel

really proud. They thought it was going to be a hippie walkover but it wasn't at all.

We put five of them in hospital; bollocks the size of footballs mainly and a broken arm I think. They said the women were the worst. It's difficult to remember the exact events, it's a bit of a blur because it was quite an emotional thing. When they actually got in, that was so heavy. We were in despair. We were running round going in front of the vehicles, getting under the vehicles and they were just coming and trashing us all the time. They were pulling us out, getting rougher and rougher so we were having to get rougher and rougher ourselves. We were doing non-violent action really, but we were forced into violence ourselves, to try and stop them from pulling us off. They were using pressure points and stuff like that. One bloke really damaged my neck and put me out. I thought I was going to die for a minute.

The police did turn up at one point but they just went away again, left us to it. It was outrageous. We kept persisting but eventually they got the fence all the way up.

The next day, the Thursday, was really bad. I didn't know they were going to come in and trash the whole woods at the bottom, but they did. We realised then that there was no chance of us stopping them. In terms of direct action in the protest, I suppose there's not much more we can do. But our plans are wider than that anyway.

We'll stay on in this forest for as long as we can then move on. We've cleared it up a bit – it's important to do that, not least so that people want you back. But it was a bit of a mess before, lots of fallen trees, a real shambles. We've cleared as much as we can – it helps it breathe and makes things grow. Now we've just got to build on what we've started with the tribe, develop a system in which we can live harmoniously and also try and educate a whole new world to that way of life.

A tribe has to have a purpose, a direction. A tribe has got to be motivated working towards something. When I was in Teepee Valley the last time it was so flat. The people there have no motivation, they're very apathetic. Probably because they grow their own weed and are stoned a lot.

When David Bellamy was down here to join the protest he called us the indigenous people of Britain. Britain is a tribal nation, that's its history, that's its roots. I feel part of that in a way that I don't feel part of normal modern society. Although I grew up in it and went through its education system, I don't feel an affinity with it. We think we can offer people a different way of living and thinking about the world. And something has got to happen. More and more people I meet, normal straight people who have jobs and all that, are so depressed, so sad and so cut off. They're just desperate to live with other people but they just haven't got the guts to go and do it. I'm saying that you can live really comfortably outdoors. You can live really well and much more holistically. Even when it comes down to shitting and pissing outdoors – it's so much more happier and healthier to do that. A lot of diseases and illnesses are caused by stress, the way houses are built and the habits and rituals people get involved in. They think it's just totally normal but it's actually the cause of their cancer. Central heating is seriously unhealthy. When you live outdoors you don't have all that. It's freer, healthier, less stressful. Our goal now is to promote that way of life as widely as we can, because it's better for people and it's better for the planet.

SPUD

Spud doesn't build the usual dome-shaped bender; just a long thin shape that looks like a big armadillo. To get in you peel back the tarps. Inside you can see the intricate turns of the hazel poles, and the hessian insulation between the wood and the plastic tarps, which seem to be the only items Spud uses which have come from the twentieth century. Inside there's a bed beside which lie three books. The top one is about spiritual healing.

The bed takes up half the space of the bender; the rest is the living area. Under the rugs there are floorboards, and under them, stone. At the far end there's a box of cooking pans, a box of vegetables and a tiny stove for cooking on. When he puts the stove on he has to leave the door open. Normally, he says, even in the middle of winter, all he needs to heat up this tiny space is the warmth of two candles. He doesn't have a radio.

The bender's been up over a year, but he left it in the summer and travelled to Scotland where friends live on a site on the Kyle of Lochalsh.

He gave up drinking a while ago, and not so long back smoking too.

The bender's on its own, a distance away from the travellers' buses parked on the Cornish cliffs, but though Spud likes his privacy, everyone seems to get on with him. He lopes around the site, helping to push cars when needed, or putting an escaped horse back into a field.

It's been misty here for three days now. Every minute or so, you can hear the foghorn a mile away at Pendeen booming mournfully, warning ships off the rocks, day and night. Spud says he doesn't even notice it any longer. In the brown light in his bender, he talks a lot about why he does things, and then stops himself and grins sheepishly. 'God, I sound like a bloody saint, don't I?'

For some reason in 1985 I had the feeling I had to go to Stonehenge and I arrived the 2nd of June, the day of the Beanfield trashing. I was twenty-four. I had A-levels and I'd started a degree in European studies, but this was like a really strange realisation for me, because suddenly it was like, 'These are my people, this is where I should be.' I found my own people and that was it. I had to be on the road.

That changed my life, but being an idiot, I didn't go on the road immediately. I thought I had to get something together first, so I went and got a job to get money to buy a vehicle, and then the same thing happened the next year too, at Stoney Cross and I lost my first vehicle, an Austin van.

I gave up vehicles in the end. I couldn't handle the pollution. Last year I went travelling with some friends of mine who'd gone horsedrawn and they said I could go along with them. I had to learn about it, and now I'm into that, but I don't think I'll go horsedrawn myself. When it comes to my own spiritual path, my own development, I have to leave everything behind. I'm going to go on foot abroad, and I suppose I might end up with a donkey, but I don't know.

I've always thought that there was something else apart from the material world that we're brought up with in school. We're consuming too much. I can't cope with that. I take myself away from the world of men and seek the kingdom of God.

I wouldn't want to live in a town. There are too many people. Towns are unhealthy. I don't like electricity, gas and all the other sort of problems. Gas, electricity, cars . . . people've only had things like that this century really. They managed OK for the previous ten thousand years.

It's not pride, me living like this, it's just got to stop. We're polluting the air that we breathe and destroying the atmosphere, and it has to stop or there won't be any future.

I do farm work, like doing the hops in Kent, but I'm getting to the point where I'm finding it really hard to do anything like that, because they're spraying the earth. I don't want to be a part of it. There's not enough organic farms to find work on.

I'm a vegetarian, mainly vegan. I'm quite weird. I try to eat as much organic stuff and as much raw stuff as possible. I don't drink tea or coffee and I try not to eat sweets, and never buy them. I think diet is one of the things that affects your general health. I feel a lot better, happier and cleaner, in particular from eating raw food. I'm not clogged up. The more you try and harmonise your body with your spirit, the more you notice the damage that other things are doing, like smoking.

After Stoney Cross I thought, 'Fuck it with this country,' and in the autumn I went to France, grape picking. I travelled there for two years. When I came back I suppose I had a nervous breakdown. I went off my head. In France everyone drinks all the time, I didn't drink before that. You're basically being passed the bottle, and I got a bit of a drink problem. When I came back I got stuck in a house in Stourbridge because I was trying to pass my driving test and get a full licence, but the alcohol got hold of me because I hated being there. So my life just revolved around drinking loads of alcohol to blot it out.

It was very difficult to give up drinking. I went to Scotland, of all places, to do it. But I was fifteen miles from the nearest village, so I just stayed on site, wooding and sitting in my bus, keeping warm, drying my clothes from the incessant rain. In the end you have to stop. It's a decision. I quite reduced it, came back here, got into it again, and went back to Scotland again and dried out. It's like smoking. You have to make a decision in the end.

I stopped for a bit in '92 at a Benedictine monastery in Brittany, and then at a Buddhist one in Scotland, but I don't believe that any organised religion has got the whole picture. They've all got part of it, but somewhere along the line they've become corrupted. I'm more of a Christian mystic than anything else.

I'm happy. I used to live in a high-rise flat before I came on the road. That was a shithole. I can look outside now and have a brilliant view, instead of looking out and seeing the West Midlands. The only thing that makes life difficult is that a large part of the population hates me. They want to prevent me having a life, through ignorance. They can burn everything I own, because I'm not into material possessions. I'll sleep out here with nothing. I can carry on for ever.

Other than that, they'll have to shoot me, and that doesn't worry me because I'm not scared of death.

PART FOUR

24-HOUR PARTY PEOPLE

RICO

Paul Simmonds is the flak catcher. He's the Travellers' Liaison Officer for Avon Council, the county with the highest density of travellers. They operate a policy of non-harassment, which means they don't automatically evict travellers who park up on council property. In fact, they often provide them with temporary sanitation facilities – Portaloos, big refuse bins and, where it's feasible, a standpipe. There are over forty of these squatted sites on council property and Paul is responsible for them all.

He's the man in the middle, trying to fashion some sort of compromise from the muddle of competing interests that come into play wherever travellers are involved: local residents, police, environmental health officers, MPs, city councillors, council welfare services, not to mention the travellers themselves. It's like juggling jelly.

It's a thankless job but it certainly has variety. Yesterday, for instance, there was an 'incident', the latest development in a long-running feud between two large families of Irish travellers. Something was on the cards when all the women from one of the families moved off their site and applied for emergency council accommodation for themselves and their children, all claiming they'd just separated from their husbands. They were obviously clearing out in anticipation of some trouble.

Then there was the recent case of the horse up at the Funny Farm on Chipping Sodbury Common, home of Circus Warp one of the major rave sound systems. One of their horses had been knocked down on the road and later died at the site. After a while they called Paul in to clear away the corpse. Paul called the knacker's yard and arranged for it to be picked up, but by the time he got there the horse had been skinned by its owner. It was now officially meat, and health and safety regulations meant the knacker couldn't touch it. He left a message with Paul explaining the situation but a mix-up between their secretaries meant that Paul didn't realise that the rotting skinned carcass hadn't been disposed of until five days later. All in a day's work.

Today it's a visit to Hanham, a site on the outskirts of Bristol where the new Avon ring-road is being constructed. It's a bleak place, made even more depressing by the presence of the Skool Bus, once a thriving playbus for kids financed by the Travellers School Charity, now unused and abandoned. The site has some familiar problems. Local residents have been systematically complaining about the mess, the noise and the nuisance caused by people on the site ever since it opened. The travellers have been banned from the local Asda after a few were suspected of shoplifting. They even pour disinfectant on the food they leave out after it's past its sell-by date so that travellers can't take it. Not like good old Marks & Sparks who set all the usable stuff to one side.

Most sinister of all is the heroin. Not everyone on the site is taking it by any means but it's rife. There's a disturbing increase in heroin use among travellers which parallels that in society at large. There was even a fatal overdose at Hanham recently.

This is not something that Rico is prepared to discuss with outsiders. Because Hanham is an officially sanctioned council site a warden has been employed to oversee it. Paul appointed Rico, an irrepressible Mancunian in his late forties, vaguely reminiscent of Compo in 'Last of the Summer Wine'. Rico has been travelling for thirteen years. His job is to make sure the site is kept reasonably tidy, to keep a record of who's staying there, to make sure the skips and toilets are emptied and the entrances and exits kept clear for emergencies.

It suits Rico. He'd have been staying there anyway. And he's quite happy to be getting paid to look after his own.

L ife goes in twelve-year cycles. I became Rico when I was thirty-six years old. I was born in the Chinese year of the monkey, when I was thirty-six it was the year of the monkey and last year was the year of the monkey.

It's time for a new cycle for me. I started travelling later than most I suppose, but we've all done it for the same reason – to escape from society. I went to art school until I was twenty, travelled round for a bit hitch-hiking and that. But I was in a bad road accident – I had to have a false hip. That stopped me working really. I got married to a woman who already had kids. The trap. No work, no nothing. We lived in a council house in Ashton-under-Lyne. Trashton-under-Slime we called it.

I started going to a few festivals just as a punter. I met people who lived in trucks and caravans and thought, 'That seems all right'. It was a choice. You could either live in a council house with fuck-all money and no respect from your neighbours because you were out of work. Or you could live in a caravan with a bunch of people you got along with who gave you a bit of respect and the opportunity to make a living, which you can do in this life if you've got a bit of brain. There's always something you can turn your hand to.

I burned my bridges. I bought an FG and a twenty-foot trailer and went to Stonehenge. That first year I mainly sold beanburgers, but at the Devil Bridge psilocybin fair, the mushroom fair, my wife did dal and chapatis and I was doing coffee. I bought a bottle of whisky and realised my profits were good. You can buy bottles of whisky in the supermarket for £8, get thirty decent-sized shots out of that for 50p each and you've got a 100 per cent mark-up.

That winter I split up with my missus. I stayed in Talley Valley then moved to the Gower peninsular, very beautiful there. I became Rico after that. I designed a new persona if you like, my festival persona. We're all more than one person – I let the personality that was necessary to run the bar develop. I took on a new character. Before, I was quieter – I was an artist, a painter, a quiet person. I had to become more outgoing, more aggressive, learn how to handle people in the bar. I started learning a lot of new things. I got into music and learned how to play the guitar and the flute. I learned tightrope walking. I learned to do a fire show. I had a quarter staff with an asbestos rope on both ends of the stick and did drum major moves and martial arts moves, the stick going really fast round the body. And fire-breathing too. It's not dangerous. It's the same technique as blowing a trumpet. If you don't blow into the wind and don't have a beard you're fine. I made a living in all sorts of ways. Rico's Coffee House & Whisky Bar was the main thing but I did engravings for people, did busking. My bar was illegal, I suppose, because it was unlicensed, but that's really petty. There was no need for the police to get involved with us lot at all. There used to be fifty thousand people at Stonehenge and we didn't need police – we police ourselves. If people are out of order it's taken care of by the people around them.

Us lot – for want of a better term, the 'new age travellers' – we've all had to make a choice about our lives. We're all people who've decided that society doesn't work for us. So we've got a home together, some sort of living space that suits us, and built some sort of business on the festival circuit – doing cafés, busking in the towns, selling stuff and, of course, some selling drugs. When I started out there was a lot of strong characters who seemed to gather together at that particular time and it was very magical. People took on roles. There were jobs needed doing for the festivals and people would just click into it. Someone would become a promoter, someone would start building a stage and find they were really good at it even though they'd never done it before, someone would get a big top together. It grows. And people become stronger for it. People find things in themselves they didn't know they had.

The spirit at festivals has always been good. Like there'd be a communal kitchen. Someone would set it up and go round the site getting the odd cabbage, the odd couple of spuds or whatever, maybe even a bit of money or a lump of hash. There'd always be a big meal come together by the end of the day.

I think the festivals probably saved a lot of people. Like the smackheads in the cities. They're trapped there;

there's nothing else for them but to carry on with it and die. When they got away to festivals everything was lighter, it gave them a break, away from the pressures of the city. I know things are changing and scag's all over the place now but I'd say the festivals have saved a lot of people's lives over the years. There are social drugs and drugs that are really bad for you. It's a big difference. There's nowt wrong with somebody smoking a bit of hash in a field, listening to a bit of rock'n'roll and having a good time – that's not hurting anybody.

And what's wrong with having a party? There's a need for it. People haven't got a lot of money. A lot of people are broke and on the dole. Does that mean they're not allowed any entertainment? Festivals have given that to people over the years. It's like these raves. I don't like rave music myself and the rave thing has fucked things up a bit for us, but there's a definite need for it. Trouble is, straight people's idea of having a party is people sitting round a front room playing parlour games.

They destroyed Stonehenge because they were frightened of us, frightened of free-thinkers who don't want to live like they do. The Beanfield happened because it was the twelfth year of the festival and if you stage a festival on the same place for twelve years you have a Royal Charter which gives you the right to have it – like the showmen have got with a lot of the established fairs. It was crucial for them to stop it that year – that's why they went to the lengths they did, dragging pregnant women through broken windscreens and all the rest of it. If they'd left us alone we'd have been OK. There'd not be all the fuss about signing on. Nobody needed to sign on then. Loads of the younger types who are coming out in trucks now, they've not got the advantage of Stonehenge. Basically, four weeks of Stonehenge used to set me up for the rest of the summer. Festivals created our own economy. Stonehenge was like a really important gateway. Stopping it hasn't stopped people coming on the road but it's stopped people doing it through a gateway where they could do it successfully – learn the ropes, get a business going.

If they spent a fraction of the money they spend hassling us to help us, maybe let us have a few sites for festivals, there wouldn't be the problems there are. In Europe they do more – in France all the military places are there for travellers to pull up on when they're not being used. They don't have all the property and trespass laws that we have here which is all to do with the history of Britain.

You get all these lords and what have you – they only own the land because their forefathers cut somebody's throat and won a battle. This chap I know up north is trying to keep places open for walkers and ramblers. He met this lord who said, 'What are you doing on my land?' My mate said, 'Well, what makes it your land?' He said his forefathers fought for it, so the fella said, 'Right, well, I'll fight thee for it.' He got beat up by the lord's lackeys and thrown off.

I see a lot of good things in our world that you don't see in Babylon – Babylon being the bigger world, the free state of Albion being us. When you're living on sites all the time there's always a division. People in Babylon separate themselves from us, we separate ourselves from them. It works both ways. They don't like us, they say we're scum.

I don't care what they say. I have standards. I'm an honest man – I'm not Ernest Saunders. There's a lot of important knowledge that we keep alive. A lot of our ladies know about herbs and herbal healing. My mate Spider knows how to make a wooden wheel – how many people know that nowadays? But most important is we try and make more of people. What's wrong with Babylon is they try and make you less, try to put you down. They make themselves look better by putting other people down. Like when people from Babylon see that I paint and draw they say, 'Oh, bit of an artist are you?' That's a real Babylonian statement, that. I'm not a bit of an artist, I'm a good artist. I'm a lot of an artist. If you fixed drains they wouldn't say, 'Bit of a plumber, are you?' or if you

fiddled rich people's taxes for a living they wouldn't say,
'Oh, bit of an accountant are you?' That's Babylon's
attitudes to us in a nutshell. Doing the warden's job here
has just made me see that more clearly.

The job's just a temporary thing. This site'll probably be
made unofficial soon and that'll be the end of it. I don't
care. It's just another step to earn some money and put
myself in a position to work on the paintings. I want to go
to Spain in April if I've got enough money. Live there for a
couple of years and get on with my work. That'll be the
next cycle for Rico.

I've got a project I want to do over the next two years –
get enough artwork together for an exhibition, tribal art of
the nineties. It'll basically be about how I've lived for the
past twelve years, about the life of us travellers. I'll have to
work hard at it. I can be good just sitting here doing bits
and pieces but with anything like art and music to com-
pete in the big world you've got to be more than good.
You've got to be brilliant. And you've got to be dedicated.
It's hard to do that when you're travelling, but I'll do it.

GARY

You can't miss Gary's place. You walk down Fairfield Road, a quiet, steeply winding residential road in the Montpelier district of Bristol, and there at the bottom is a big yellow coach with a trailer box attached. Both are decorated with stars and circus tents painted in red, and signs advertising Gary's business, RAINBOW MARQUEES.

Inside is an immaculately tailored home, varnished wood throughout – a sleeping area for himself at the back, bunks for his three children in the middle section, a shower, a wall-mounted water heater, a kitchen area and at the front a table with two benches that'll sit six at a pinch. Leaning against the back of the seat there's a sweeping brush and a guitar.

It's lit by an oil lamp. On a shelf next to the table is Gary's tape machine. Gary may be in his forties but he keeps up to date with his music. Chumbawumba and Radical Dance Faction (RDF) – the big festival favourites – are at the top of the pile.

He lives here with three of his children who all attend the local primary school. They get on fine there because, as he says, 'this area's full of bohemian types'.

He could be Keith Richards's twin brother – the same unkempt seventies haircut, the same haggard, lined face, the same mischievous glint in his eye, the same rogueish charm.

His jumper is more Gyles Brandreth in his TV-AM days – a dazzling riot of primary colours. He's teamed it with a pair of skin-tight leggings in purple and orange stripes.

He has a lot of visitors. He likes to sit there, rolling his cigarettes and telling his stories.

In 1980 I went to my first Stonehenge and that changed everything. I was on the fringes of that sort of thing anyway. I was interested in eastern religions and ecology, looking for a better way of being. But I was a bit lost; didn't know exactly where I was going.

I'd been married with a couple of kids and separated. I'd been working and earning pretty good money – £400, £500 doing plumbing and heating engineering which in the seventies was pretty good money. I'd lived in Wales in a caravan for a while but I met a lady and moved back to London with her.

I went to Stonehenge just for a weekend and decided I was going to come back the next year ready to travel proper. I screwed up the relationship with the lady I'd come back to London with and moved to a place called Bradford on Avon. It was there that I met a man who made teepees. I bought myself a teepee and a van and learned how to do leather craftwork. I started making moccasins to measure, street moccasins with hard soles. I was ready for my first Stonehenge proper. Stonehenge was about freedom. The freedom to actually blossom the way you wanted to blossom, to do what you wanted to do as long as it didn't hurt anybody else. It was far out.

New age travellers of the seventies and early eighties were driven by visions, ideals, inspiration. The influx of what I would call economic refugees has changed it completely. They're driven by desperation basically and they haven't got the ideals that drove us on the road looking for something better. What they're doing now is driving on to travellers' sites all the shit of the city.

It's what went wrong with Stonehenge as well. The breadheads came in and it was all about how much money they could make selling drugs. Stonehenge was about getting high but you didn't need to take loads and loads of drugs getting high at Stonehenge – you got high on the vibrations . . . and freedom . . . and life. So incredibly high. You could stay awake for days on it without taking any speed, without taking acid, just bubbling all the time. There was a spiritual energy in the air, something difficult to explain. Maybe it's the place itself? Maybe it's the people there wanting to be free and to love one another.

I stay away from festivals now. I fear them. I don't want to get my home trashed. I don't want flak from the Old Bill.

After Stonehenge I followed the festival around. We went to Inglestone Common, up to East Anglia, the Norwich Free, a dinky little festival just outside Norwich with a tiny stage and only about twenty, twenty-five vehicles there. Very friendly. We all got to know each other really well over a period of about three or four weeks. There was a little pond there which we could swim and bathe in. And the locals would come along at night, listen to our sounds and buy our wares. That year I sold all my plumbing tools, so it would be difficult for me to go back to my old life even if I was tempted.

I'd met up with people from Talley Valley over the year. They'd invited me to come and winter there and that's what I did.

The second year I went to Stonehenge I worked with a café called Pressed Rat & Warthog, Pink Floyd characters I believe. I was doing wholewheat pancakes filled with various fillings from jams and lemon and sugar and stuff to a hash treat, with hash fudge inside the pancake. After that I went back to Talley Valley. All this time I'm splitting with ladies and making with ladies, making children and all that.

Life was so much easier then. There was practically no hassle from the police, we could keep ourselves together. I think the state had always feared us, but they went over the top at Windsor in '74. They decided to chuck everybody off in a dawn raid, busting heads and what have you. They got a lot of bad press over it. Hippies were flower children at that time, remember. What they'd done was seen as being very uncool and they were forced to give us a site the next year.

In the end the reason they were able to get into the festivals again and bust the festivals up was that they became more drug-orientated. Eventually we had the *News of the World* in and pictures in the press of drug signs at Stonehenge, people advertising the drugs they were selling. It changed the tone of the festival. It attracted more and more people. But by casting its net wider it was accepting a different kind of person; people who were attracted by the drugs that were available there as much as anything else.

In '83 I started my own café with a teepee up on one pole and spread wide so it was open. Later on during the year I got an awning stretched out and held up with brightly coloured poles. I did mushroom tea and hash cakes. It was the first time I'd resorted to selling drugs. I OKed that in my head because I'd worked on the drugs, turning them into hash cakes, making tea and providing an ambient space where people could come and munch out.

I was very attracted to a group called the Tibetan Ukraine at that time, one of the first circus groups. They had a band, jugglers, a very loose show. Very magical. By the end of the '83 season my lodge was across the track from them and we were getting to know each other well. I decided I wanted to be a part of it. Their marquee had had it and they were obviously going to need a new one. My plan to get into the Tibetan Ukraine was to turn up the next year with a new marquee for them. I wanted to be invited to join, I didn't want to have to ask. I wanted to go in as an equal. I got myself a coach, resprayed it in rainbow colours and set about getting canvas and designing a marquee.

I went to see the guy who'd built my first teepee for me and got some hints off him on how to design. I went away and worked on the design and decided what I needed. I'd built my own teepee by that time so I had some canvas experience. I met a lady who fronted me £1,000 and I built it. It was red and yellow waterproof canvas – the Tibetan colours – round, with a centre pole, about forty foot in diameter. It went up the first time at Stonehenge. We'd never tried it before then, it took us right up until the last minute to build it. I cut the poles myself from trees in the forest, stripping the bark off, smoothing them. Finishing the canvas ended up taking all winter. We got there two days before the solstice. We arrived in the afternoon, found our site and decided to wait until dark, to put the marquee up in the middle of the night so it would blow people's minds when they woke up in the morning and saw it.

It wasn't all good, though. I fell out with Chris, the chap who'd helped me build it. He laboured for me and thought that entitled him to run the fucking thing. I ended up buying him out but he stayed on the fringes of my group and wheeled and dealed and played mind games and it resulted in the tent being taken off me by him and his friends, with the backing of the so-called Peace Convoy. We went from Stonehenge to Montgomery that year and it was at Montgomery that the shit started to hit the fan. Chris wasn't working with me; he was trying to do things on his own and the payment he'd taken for his labour was my generator. I didn't get to join the Tibetan Ukraine – someone had got there before me with another marquee and they were going to be there till the end of the summer, by which time Tibet would be looking for a new marquee. So that didn't come off and I didn't have a generator. By the end of Montgomery things had got pretty bad. What I didn't know was that Chris had been talking behind my back and had actually got into the lady's head who had put the money forward.

I went to take the tent down the morning after a windstorm – the tent was looking pretty droopy and the festival was finished. I was taking it down and I got told to stop by some bod that I'd never met before. We ended up having a punch-up. Then I got told by a group of people that it was in the hands of a Wally – a Wally being one of the original groups from Stonehenge – and that he was going to be the keeper of the marquee until the ownership was sorted out. I left Montgomery and went up to Pickup

Bank in Lancashire where it was decided that I would run
the stage and Chris would run the café inside. The problem was that Chris and I were no longer a unit and he's
running the café which makes all the money and I'm
operating the stage which makes sweet fuck-all. All the
dealers are around me making heaps and heaps of
money. I'm refusing to let dealers deal from inside the
marquee and refusing to have anything to do with drug
dealing myself. I wanted the marquee kept clean. I got
money by passing a bucket round during performances
by bands or juggling acts or whatever, and by seeing the
various tradesmen round and about me who I was attracting custom for through the marquee. Some of the dealers
offered me drugs as my commission. I refused as it would
mean I would have to become a drug seller to get the
capital to keep me going. Things worked pretty well,
though. I was actually working a little bit underhand. I
was really sick of the way the festival thing was going
with the drugs and the way I'd had my thing stopped by
people who were part of that. I wanted to be away from
them. I wanted to be with a together group of travellers –
craftsmen, artists, entrepreneurs. I wanted to get something together like a travelling craft fair. I worked behind
the scenes talking to the more together travellers about
doing that, about splitting away from the main so-called
Peace Convoy. I imagine that's what rubbed some people
up the wrong way.

   But at the end of Pickup Bank the marquee was loaded
back on to my bus, and the sound equipment and everything else. People had seen that I ran a good tight show –
much better than it had been with Chris trying to do
it – and were feeling good about working alongside me.
I wasn't happy about travelling with them but we were
going to the same place from there on in, a green festival
up in Cumbria.

   A small group of vehicles – including myself, the marquee and my crew, the people who helped me put the tent
up – were going up ahead of the main convoy to secure a
position on the site for the marquee before everyone else

got there, and to plan out the site. The rest of the lead
vehicles were on the road waiting for me, I was the last to
come off. They were parked down the side of the road so I
could go in front and lead the way. I was the flagship; I
was brightly painted, in pristine condition, with the king
pole on the roof like an arrow.

As I drove off down the road past them, gathering
speed, my steering went totally out of control. I slid down
the side of three or four vehicles and ended up in a ditch.

What happened next seemed to be very well co-
ordinated. Chris came steaming through the door – his
had been one of the vehicles I'd hit. I'd done minor
damage to them but the damage to my own bus was
terrible, all along the front wing and the door was a wreck.
I was sitting dazed in the seat. He steamed in, pulled me
out of my seat and started whacking me. At one stage he
picked up a lump of metal and it looked like he was going
to push it into my face. He had second thoughts about
that and pushed it through my windscreen instead. He
threw me out the door, jumped on me, kicked me in the
head and left me pretty dazed on the ground. His mates
are running up and down the side of the coach with
crowbars putting the windows through. Then they came
on the coach, took the sound equipment, took the tent,
took the king pole off the roof, took everything and left
me smashed on the side of the road. They left.

The rest of the convoy left an hour or so later, with just a
small group left on site to clear up as always. We were
pretty tidy in those days. We had time to be. The police
weren't hassling us quite so much to leave sites quickly.

I spent the next three days fixing my vehicle up so I
could at least drive it. We inspected the damage, looking
for what had caused the steering to go out of control and
found that the track rod was bent into a V-shape. It had a
kink in the centre of it, a pressure kink where somebody
had put, we think, a crowbar underneath the axle, and
distorted the tracking. I hadn't noticed it when I was
driving across the rough ground of the site, you're always

bumping all over the place, wheels spinning. But as soon as I got on the road it had lost control. It was sabotage.

It's quite a powerful position to be in, running a tent like that. And when you're the top of a pyramid, there's a lot of people that want to knock you down. Chris wanted that control and that power. He was heavily into speed as it turned out. I got repaired and went up to the festival after my marquee. When I got there I was told that it was now the People's Marquee. I was injured, man. And I was shocked. My whole fucking world had been dissolved by this happening, you know. I just said, I don't accept it, but I'm not going to argue about it. It's mine. I built it. I designed it. The money was given to me, no strings attached. It's mine.

I went away, went back to Wales and got myself a new bus, the one I've got now. The convoy went from the Cumbrian festival to a place called Nostell Priory near Leeds. That's where the convoy first got trashed by the police. I don't really know the truth of what happened there to this day. I heard Chris killed a police dog. I know he got busted. For LSD. Hundreds of them. He ended up going down for three years.

I was back in Wales when one day a friend turned up and told me where the marquee had been taken and stashed for the winter. It was a site about twenty-five miles from where I was living. I and some friends of mine – respected ethnic 'new age' people rather than convoy-type travellers, Talley Valley teepee-people whose barn I'd used to build the marquee – went down and assured the farmer who was keeping it that I was the rightful owner. He said he'd agreed to hold it for someone else but he'd give them twenty-four hours to come and argue the toss. They never turned up and we collected it the next day. I left the country then. I was sick of it. I'd had it up to there. I wanted out. I'd given everything I had to an ideal which I really believed in. I'd worked my bollocks off. And I'd been beaten up for it; and robbed; and slandered. I felt very, very hurt.

I got a phone call from Nik Turner of Hawkwind who informed me that the Tibetan Ukraine were now in the South of France at a free new circus event. It started on my birthday so I just thought, 'Fuck, it's a birthday party for me, I'm going.' I went off to the South of France with the marquee for the Tibetan Ukraine and travelled with them for the next three or four months in France, through the Pyrenees, to Biarritz and into Spain – San Sebastian. We parted company with them when they went off to Portugal – me, Mandy, the lady I was with, her child, the baby that was in her belly which we'd conceived in Talley Valley a few months before.

We motored down through Madrid, Granada, to the Mediterranean and Malaga. Got into Malaga and had an accident, wrote off a Ford Fiesta. All the cash went in the process. Things were pretty tough. I ended up selling my blood to make sure that my lady and unborn were properly fed. I'd learnt how to juggle and slowly got a busking trip together. I bought Mandy a puppet and she played a tin whistle. We started busking, although it was more like begging at first. We weren't very good, we had no make-up and no costumes. But slowly it came together and by the time we got to Barcelona some four months later we must have been about the highest paid buskers there. Not because we were the best but because we looked good – if you have a child and a pregnant woman you get money out of people's pockets. We'd get £15 to £20 for a twenty-minute stint, Friday and Saturday afternoons when people have money. That would pay for the week. It was really good, probably the best year of my life.

We came home to Britain because my father was ill and I wanted to be with him. He took a long time to die.

I was going to college up until then. I had this idea that I wanted to be a teacher and I found a teacher training college in Ambleside where they did an outdoor education course, environmental science and pursuits. My father died halfway through the second term which made the course a bit wobbly. He left me a packet of money which enabled me to build a four-pole big top.

I was married to Mandy by that time; we had three kids together plus hers, living in a cottage in Coniston. But the relationship was fizzling out, finished. We'd actually met at Stonehenge in '84 before the shit hit the fan with the marquee and started living together then, so it had lasted five years.

Then in the summer of 1989 I met a young lady named Toni. She was just coming on eighteen, twenty years younger than me, and she blew my head away. I went back to college for one more term after the summer, but wanted to travel again. I'd found what I'd come to Cumbria for and it wasn't a fucking teaching degree. I wanted to go and do circus now. I decided I wanted to build a bigger tent and designed this four-pole big top based on the sacred geometry of Stonehenge and the pyramids. I tried to square the circle, which is an alchemist term. The actual design of the marquee was based on the size of the circles of Stonehenge. The four king poles with the circumference drawn through their centre was the size of the inner circle at Stonehenge. It was a strange-shaped tent. The outer circle of the circumference of the tent was the circumference and diameter of the second circle of Stonehenge. I had an extension – some of the triangles that made up the circle were longer, like a fishtail coming off the round four-pole top for a stage area and at the edge of that, the poles were the dimension of the next circle of Stonehenge. How I squared the circle was by building a pyramid that sat on top of the four king poles.

I got a partner, Simon, because I needed more money than I had. He came in with me as a one-third partner for donating half the money – we put in four and a half grand each. I'd been to see the Glastonbury festival organisers by that time and taken them photographs of a scale model that I'd built and got them to hire both my tents for the next festival. We got it built just in time and opened up on the Saturday morning.

We had a good time there – bands in the big marquee, an African drum workshop which went on twenty-four hours a day for three days just on the other side of the field.

I already had another booking in Barrow-in-Furness for August. We went up to a farm in Lancashire where we rehearsed a show and worked on our equipment then went up to Barrow on 7 August for this gig. The next day it rained. Water was coming through the canvas. Now, I'd bought the canvas off a firm in Dundee who hadn't been able to supply me off the shelf with flame retardant waterproof canvas in the colours I wanted, red and yellow. We'd had it shipped down to Norfolk to be treated. The fucking firm that did it, didn't do it. They've gone bust now and he's been done but I still haven't got my money back. It's taken two and a half years. For all that time I've taken round this tent that I still can't use. I've had to sell the little marquee to settle my bills. Since then we've been trying to get things together. We worked for a while for Snap Dragon Circus and Toni's been doing more training. I've been working on plans for another circus and squabbling with the council.

I've had enough of being hounded from pillar to post by the rednecks. I want out of this country. The shit's going to hit the fan soon anyway. We're planning to go to France and travel there. Every traveller who's got his head screwed on is heading out now. The country's going to go pop pretty soon anyway with the economic situation as it is. I don't want to be in the city when that happens.

What's happening in Eastern Europe will happen here. Our economies aren't really in much better shape, they've just got a better front. I want to be somewhere where I've got a chance. I'm heading for south-west France, good climate, low population. If things go pop I can live off the land. I'm a teepee person. It's a very good training. We'll be the people who survive.

VIC

Vic and Jeremy are between trucks. She's sold hers, he's sold his and they're in the process of buying a bigger, better one. There's a slight dispute. Assured that it was in good running order they agreed a price of £1,000 with the woman selling it, but it has since failed its MOT and they want a discount or the necessary repairs done. Vic's got to sort this all out while Jeremy's on tour in Europe with his group The Levellers. She's also busying herself cutting pictures of Keanu Reeves out of magazines and sticking them all over the flat. It's a joke for when Jeremy comes home. He'll get it.

They've been renting a flat in Brighton for a few months while they sorted themselves out. It's been a hectic year for both of them. They've only been going out properly for a few months and they wanted to be alone for a while, to have a bit of peace, just them and the two dogs, Grim Dog and Trebor. It's the first time either of them have ever lived legally in a flat or house since fleeing the parental nest. They think it's a waste of money: all that rent; gas bills; electricity bills. It's not worth it. They're itching to get back on the road, but want to live a bit more calmly from now on. They'll take the bus with them to wherever Jeremy's recording the next Levellers album and when he's not on duty with the band they'll travel and park up with their friends Scott and Jane. They have a hazy notion that they might live in a houseboat one day but at the moment all they can think of is getting that truck and getting back on the road. They want to be out by April.

I suppose it's always been in my nature to be restless, to move around and never live in the same place for long.

I've never really had any roots. I'm not really from any-where. My parents never lived anywhere for more than about two years – they're like me, can't seem to settle anywhere, not very good with jobs and things like that. I decided to leave home five years ago when I was fifteen. Me and this bloke were living in a tent because we didn't have anywhere to live. I met his best friend who was a student in Birmingham – he said I could go and live with him there and I ended up going out with him. It didn't work well – he was a very studenty type, I wasn't really into that kind of thing.

I met these traveller types, more squatters really, living in trucks and really horrible squats, not together squats at all but places with no water, no leccy. One of them called Pinner – I used to think he worked down on a coalmine, he was so dirty all the time. I was so naive, I suppose. I never understood why they were so dirty so I just pre-sumed they must work down a mine or something until I went back to their trucks with them one day.

Basically we just used to go down the pub all the time. We'd just spend all day there. And because I spent all my time with them this boy finished with me. I went off with them in their truck one day to Nottingham. I was meant to have been doing an A-level that morning and I rang him up from Nottingham and said, 'Hey, we're in Nott-ingham, it's great,' and he just said, 'Don't bother coming back.'

When he kicked me out I had nowhere to live so I kipped in these squats for a while. We used to sleep rough a lot as well, mainly just outside the pub when we couldn't be bothered to walk home at night. They were parked behind a row of houses in Moseley. Birmingham doesn't really sound the sort of place that travellers would want to live but Moseley Village, where all the squats are, is a really nice place, like a village inside a city with trees and parks. I was seventeen by then and that was the first year I went to Glastonbury, did the festivals and got into travelling.

Pinner, the bloke I was going out with, had a little Bedford, a really old thirty-seater bus. The windscreen had been smashed so it was a real nightmare to drive when we went on the road to go to the festivals, bloody freezing – the wind coming in through this windscreen, us all huddled at the back in duvets, it was awful.

I'd never been to a festival before. I'd always lived right out in the country or up north where there aren't really many festivals. I just thought it was really weird. Muddy. That's the first impression I got: all the mud. And it was hectic. I'd never seen so many police before and I'd never seen so many drugs. I didn't take any drugs. I just used to drink all the time. I'd never seen teepees before. They had a big teepee field at Pilton that year and I thought that was really weird, people living in things like that. I couldn't get my head round that at all. I've never been a very sociable person but I enjoyed just walking round and meeting loads of people. I just used to have a really good time, staggering around being pissed. I really liked it – I was well up for it, it was just such a good laugh.

I loved the live bands, which it was more about then. It was when raves were just starting up and there were raves but it was more about bands really, especially the travellers' stage at Glastonbury. That's when I first saw the Levellers. I actually met Jeremy for the first time and thought, 'Ooh, he's really nice.' Two years later I ended up going out with him. I just thought the whole thing was really exciting – all the people, I'd never seen so many people gathered together before. It was great. And there was none of this trendy thing. Over the last couple of years it's become really trendy to be a traveller, or to be a squatter. And people who've been on the road for years have become quite snobbish about it. There wasn't any of that then. And it was something really new to me. If I'd said to any of my school friends or whatever, 'Oh, I'm living in a truck with a load of blokes with dreads,' they'd have thought it was a bit weird and horrible, but now you hear about it all the time. It's quite a trendy thing.

But I got quite ill that summer. I wasn't old enough to sign on and I was just begging and stuff. The group of people I was with looked after me, but not really very well. They were just drinking and taking drugs all the time. Food wasn't much of a priority for them. After the festival season we ended up down in Brighton and my mum and dad had just moved there a couple of months before so I ended up going to see them. I was really ill. I had to go into hospital for malnutrition. They'd seen all the stuff about the travellers and festivals on the news. My mum thought it was quite exciting and quite nice. It'd come on the telly and she'd say, 'Oh, is that your friends?' They didn't try and stop me doing it.

After that I moved to Nottingham. I used to go begging quite a lot with my friend Lou, about a year and a half ago now when I was really disgustingly crustie. I used to enjoy begging. She would stand there with her penny whistle and the boyfriend I was with then, Daz, used to juggle. I'd stand on the other side of the road just begging, but I always seemed to get more money than them. Probably because I was just a bit more vocal, I had a bit of a patter, a bit of a story how I've got to feed my dogs or my housing benefit hasn't come through, which was a big lie because I was living in squats and not paying rent. It used to give me something to do as well – going to town begging was better than just sitting around all day doing nothing. You'd get talking to people and some people were really nice, giving you food and things. If I went begging with the dogs people would come and give me tins of dog food. I didn't actually realise it was illegal. I was never arrested but I asked someone once for some money, he gave me two quid and then said, 'Actually, I'm a plain-clothes policeman and what you're doing's illegal, you better go now.'

I've been moved on quite a lot begging in London, but begging there's horrible anyway, there's just too much of it. You get a lot more abuse down there: 'Get a job', 'Dirty cow', things like that. But you get used to that. I've been beaten up just for looking like a crustie. Me and my ex-boyfriend Daz were begging in Nottingham once, really pissed up outside this club. He must have been mouthing off to someone because this huge bouncer from this other club round the corner, about eighteen stone with these six Asian guys, popped up from nowhere and beat the crap out of us. The bouncer, a big white guy, beat me up really badly. But you get a lot of that abuse in Nottingham. At the time we were the perfect crustie couple I suppose. I'm a naturally untidy, scruffy person and Daz was really dirty and scruffy but it just seemed to suit him – you couldn't imagine him any other way. For a while I was all right just travelling on my own, without a vehicle, just meeting up with other groups of travellers and kipping on other people's trucks. When I met Daz and started going out with him it got more awkward. He had two dogs, and I had two dogs so we had four dogs and accumulated quite a lot of tat as well. It became impossible to move around, so we saved up and bought the truck.

My first truck was a minibus with a BMC A Series engine. I paid £700, quite a lot really. Looking back I wouldn't have paid that much money for it – they're good trucks for doing long distances but you have to use them all the time to make it worthwhile. I ripped all the seats out, put a bed in, put a cooker in, put wood round the side, tongue-and-groove panels – a bit of a cliché, a real stereotypical traveller-truck thing to do, but it's really good insulation.

It's a whole different ball game when you own your own vehicle. In a way it becomes more difficult. There's all the legal side of it, the maintenance, finding somewhere to park. Turning up in a new town and not knowing where to park there can be a real pain. Once we went to Liverpool presuming that there must be a site there somewhere – loads of people used to park up on the Wirral over the river. We got there and there was no one there, absolutely nowhere to park in the whole city, so we had to leave. You end up having to ask the police, which is a bit ironic but they're the only people you can ask. I've done that loads of times. We even got a police escort once, to a site near Glastonbury called Ivythorne. Luckily they didn't drive us right on to the site or we wouldn't have been too popular.

Daz knew people up in Bradford so we went up there. There's a lot of parking spaces up there behind squats and things or just normal houses. You couldn't ever do that in somewhere like Brighton but you can up north because people just don't care. They're not so nosy and snobby as they are down here. There's a big Asian community in Bradford and people like that don't tend to ask questions or wonder why there's a big truck parked behind their house. It doesn't bother them. It's friendlier and people seem to be nicer. And you don't get all that cosmic, hippie stuff up north, which suits me.

Mainly, people just like getting pissed, the brew crew image is still really strong up there. When we went down to Cornwall from Birmingham my friend Boop, he's got this old BBC outside broadcast truck with BBC on the side and everyone was making jokes about how it stood for Birmingham Brew Crew. That's the kind of image people down south seem to have of northerners, real crustie: dreadlocks, ripped-up jeans. It's true in a way – they don't give a fuck – but I find them far more friendly. They seem to be more practical, really into their vehicles and into having a good time. If you go on to a site round here, for instance, people can be really snooty – don't talk to you for three days and maybe then ask you to leave unless you show a great interest in crystals.

I suppose the site I was on in Bradford would be termed brew crew. That's what we did all the time, get pissed, party. But even though the attitude was not giving a fuck about anything, having nothing to do with society at all, at the same time they'd get on with everyone.

The travellers and all the punks and squatters used to go down to the One In Twelve, a punk club. We had a pool team and we'd play matches every night against normal lad pubs and old codgers' pubs. Everyone would get on really well. There was none of that, 'Ugh, we hate you weirdoes' attitude. Probably because it was a working-

class area and they just took us for what we were, the
urban underclass trying to make a life for ourselves, and
they kind of respected us for it. There's no mystique about
living in a truck for me, it just makes sense from a practical
point of view. I'm tight-fisted and it saves money. And I
hate that attitude a lot of the hippie types have that you
have to do without – that if you've got a telly and a video
in your truck there's something wrong with you. They
say, 'You shouldn't have a telly, you'll get sucked in.'
Pathetic. I've always had a telly in my truck. We're getting
a new truck and when we live in there we'll have a
generator, telly, video, music, all that.

I suppose there is a big divide between the more punky
types and the cosmic travellers. I don't really have a lot of
time for the hippie stuff, probably because I'm a real
cynic. I'm not into that kind of mysticism. I blame my
boyfriend's band, actually, for that romantic idea of travellers that's built up; young kids have this image of buses
painted like Romany caravans, people sitting round
communal campfires. Anyone who's been on the road
knows that's a load of bollocks.

Travelling is just a good way to live in practical terms.
It's cheaper, you get to move around, go where you want
to go, do what you want to do. And you do genuinely feel
that you're living outside of society, which is what I want.

I'm a very anti-social person. Everybody in Brighton
knows me as the most miserable woman in Brighton. I
don't make friends easily. And I find society at large really
twisted and warped. I'm one of the only people I know
who's really proud to be working class. But the whole
thing running through the working class in Britain is that
they're ashamed of themselves and they think they
should always be trying to succeed, to get on and improve
themselves. I don't see why. That's what society's all
about, having to prove yourself and be successful. What
for? I don't want to prove myself to anybody. I don't want
to be like everybody else.

I'm an inverted snob as well – not something I'm
especially proud of but I can't help it. These travellers you

get called Giles, whose dads are bank managers and things, I do resent them. I worked in a factory for a while when I was sixteen and I didn't think it was beneath me. There's nothing wrong with a bit of hard work and I'll do it as and when I need to. I'd do it now if I wanted the money for some reason.

A lot of these people, the more middle-class travellers, they'd never dream of getting a job like that. They're the ones who tend to end up being the big drug dealers – and they always have the nicest trucks, their mums and dads lend them the money. I'm not saying that everyone who comes from a middle-class background is like that – I like some of them; the ones who have that naivety and want to get on with everyone and genuinely treat everyone else as their equal. But some of them are different. They're the ones who become traveller snobs, 'Oh, I've been doing it longer than you.' And they're the people who go through all the different phases of being a traveller, who've gone through the crustie bit of having dreads and stuff and who've now shaved their hair and become Spiral Tribe types, hanging round with Spiral Tribe and going to raves and that. London's full of people like that. I mean, that's really travelling isn't it, being parked up in Brixton the whole year round. And they do these squat raves and charge £4, £5 to get in. All they seem to be interested in is making money. Everyone's a punter in their eyes, someone to make money off. Those are the kind of people I resent. And I know most of them. Wankers. In fact I hit one of their girlfriends the other week. She really wound me up. Silly cow. She's one of these trendy ones – used to hang round with Chris from RDF, now she's shaved her hair and hangs round with ravers because it's trendier.

I suppose I'm a bit disillusioned with it all at the moment. Maybe it's getting older. It was really great when I first started travelling but I was seventeen then, so of course it was a good laugh – I didn't care about anything. But I'm disillusioned with this rave thing, how it's all about people just wanting to make money. And I'm disillusioned with the way everyone's become disillusioned, if you see what I mean. The apathy that's spreading at the moment. I can't stand that. Like the Skool Bus thing. What a good idea, so much potential there and it's just sitting there rusting away in Bristol. That's sad. I can understand the reasons for all this apathy, though. It is hard to keep going when everything seems to be against you. Things like that big media campaign in the summer; being moved on by the police all the time; when it spreads to the public and they start hating you. That does your head in. And drugs is a big factor. Hard drugs, heroin's a lot cheaper and a lot more readily available and that's a big factor. I wonder if that's something that's been deliberately done by the government. It's very convenient for them to have so many people using heroin; it keeps them quiet. All these drugs clinics seem to be springing up everywhere providing people with needles. And when was the last time you saw those anti-heroin adverts on the telly?

I'm getting a bit fed up of festivals too. I'll carry on going to a few because you get to see people you haven't seen for ages, but the excitement's wearing off for me. I had an awful time at Castlemorton. I just sat in the back of the truck and watched telly the whole time. I sold a lot of beer, though, which is what I do at festivals – cook meals and sell beer.

But we'll still travel. When me and Jeremy buy this truck we'll move into it. The flat was just a break for us really: Jeremy wasn't really sure what he was going to be doing and I'd had a really hectic year on the road. I split up with Daz; I got pregnant and had a miscarriage. I think that was from driving constantly all the time, stress because I was arguing with Daz all the time and getting moved on all the time, the whole thing. I've got loads of court summons at the moment. Driving without a licence and I knocked down someone's garden wall in Glastonbury. The truck was insured but that was invalid because I haven't got a licence. It was funny because after I'd done it I pulled up on site and told a few people about it. They asked where it was and about three other people had knocked down exactly the same wall. There used to be a site down this alleyway and you can't turn round when you get to the end – the site's gone now – so you have to reverse out. You can't see what you're doing and because it's on a slight slope I slipped out of gear and rolled backwards. I just brushed it going at 0.0000001 miles an hour and the whole thing collapsed. And within ten minutes they had all these people round building a new one. I reckon they do it all the time for some insurance scam. I gave them my name and that's how I got done for not having a licence. My name was on all the documents. But I got loads of producers this summer – where the police stop you and you end up having to go down the station with all your motoring documents. I doubt if it'll go to court – I just put all the court summonses back in the postbox. I had a couple of driving lessons once but that was it. I'm still a better driver than Jeremy, though – he's useless. It's actually easier driving a truck because people get out of your way. We've got a car as well and I get really scared driving that. It feels really small and vulnerable. I wouldn't mind being an HGV lorry driver, actually, but it costs quite a lot to have the lessons and take the test. I can't wait to get that new truck.

JEREMY

Rock stars with a couple of decent-selling albums under their belts tend to operate at the pricier end of the market when they're buying a new home. Not Jeremy, bass player with The Levellers. He's spotted this truck parked on a scrap of British Rail land next to his mate Scott's trailer and he reckons it's just the ticket.

Of all the groups who've built up a solid following playing regularly at travellers' festivals – Chumbawumba, Radical Dance Faction (RDF), Back to the Planet, Ozric Tentacles – it's the Levellers who've broken through into the mainstream market first and most successfully. Jeremy says it's not that they're any better than the other groups, but that they always supplemented their festival activities with dates at any club, college or squat that would have them. They've built up a loyal fan base. They have top forty singles, top ten albums, tours in America and they're expected to get even bigger when they release their next album in 1993.

The Levellers have never strayed too far from their roots. The centrepiece of their last LP was a song called 'Battle Of The Beanfield'; their biggest hit, 'One Way', is pretty much an anthem for the travellers' life. Jeremy sports the archetypal traveller/crustie look: long dreaded hair, combat trousers, army boots. On stage he's the wild energetic showman, leaping about all over the place. In real life he's quiet, with none of the self-confidence and arrogance you'd expect in a successful young rock musician. He's open, honest and chatty, but his conversation is punctuated with nervous giggles. He looks a bit bashful when the Levellers' 'One Way' comes belting out of the pub speaker. He's been sat here an hour now, nursing a single glass of grapefruit *juice. He doesn't touch a drop of alcohol these days. He says he drank his life's share in the past few years and it all got a bit too much.*

U p until 1985 I'd always thought festivals were really shit – old hippie things, nothing to do with anything I was into. Then I saw all the stuff on the telly about the battle of the Beanfield and was really interested in it because all these people looked the same way I did. I was at art school in Brighton, living in squats and that, with all these big ideas about living outside of society. As far as I could see, these people were actually doing what I was busy talking about. At the Urban Free Festival in Brighton the next year, 1986, there were a lot of travelling types there. I went to see what they were up to and began making a few friends amongst travelling people. I've been a sort of part-time traveller ever since.

Instead of just staying on the dole, I started busking about the same time; everyone was always out busking or begging, and I didn't fancy begging so busking it was. I'd earn a bit of money and go up on site and drink for a few days. I was still busking around Brighton right up to last year, actually.

I didn't get my own vehicle until a couple of years ago; before then I was just blagging spaces on people's buses or dossing down in benders made by friends because I never got round to learning how to make a bender. I got my first truck when I could afford it. It cost £600. By the time I got it, though, the band was getting really busy so I hardly ever lived on site in it except for the few days here and there that we took off. The festivals were exciting, just seeing everything come to fruition. We'd stay in a certain place and live there for a while and get this little sort of society together that actually works, devoid of any help from the government or social security. It happens. I suppose it happens in the way things always happen with human beings when they've had to happen, before governments and all that existed.

It's not trying to hark back to the past – that's something we get criticised for all the time, especially the band – but if you look at a travellers' site it does look a bit archaic. And it did sort of operate like some kind of archaic society. It was feudal law: if you take something you get hit, so you don't take anything. And it was communal. People that can cook cook. People that can play music play music. I don't know how it ever worked but it really did.

One of the best was this site we lived on just outside Amsterdam. It was a massive site, bigger than any I've seen in England and it was all centred round a bar that was open twenty-four hours a day. That was the financial hub and it was all shady dealings, drugs mainly. We were invited over there for St Patrick's night so we went and played three gigs, but it was so good we just stayed on with RDF for about three months. We did some busking and made quite a lot of money compared to what we were used to. The Mutoid Waste Company built the mixing tower and a stage out of pallets. After the gig was done someone took the mixing tower and used it as a house. The stage became a hotel – it was nine feet high, sixty feet long, forty feet deep and people who were just visiting paid a bit to kip in there. People would go out busking, food would be cooked for the people who lived there and the rest sold and it would tick over like that. Quite a solid anarcho-capitalist operation. Pretty soon after we left the whole site got bulldozed at about four o'clock one morning by the city council. Apparently they had to commandeer just about every bulldozer in Amsterdam.

I suppose there's a bit of a divide between people like me and my friends and the older, more hippie types. I don't really know many of that type and of the ones I have met I couldn't really tolerate the hippieness. They probably couldn't tolerate us, which is fair enough. I was pissed all the time. We were brewheads basically.

When I first started doing it, the basic thing was that you were totally in control of your destiny, totally independent, totally outside normal society. We were proud that no one would come anywhere near us. People were scared to even look at us. It's different now because there's been so much about travellers in the news it's quite a familiar sight, but a few years ago people would see a load of travellers coming down the street and they'd cross the road, keep out of the way; because you look ridiculous and you obviously look really threatening. I quite liked that then. I'm not like that any more and most of the people I know aren't. Nowadays we're all trying to create a better understanding between normal people and us lot.

People called us crusties and that label's stuck and become a sort of fashion thing which is ridiculous really because it was the opposite of that. It wasn't a cohesive group. And it certainly wasn't some sort of youth cult that relied on buying the right records and the right clothes and being sold things. It was anti-fashion, anti-image – wearing the cheapest, most comfortable things and not caring what you looked like. It was supposed to be a viable alternative way of life. It's difficult trying to analyse it now because at the time I just did it. I liked the people and to me it was the end of the road I was taking, it was the most extreme I could get and that was the attraction.

It revolved around drinking and drugs. The people I was hanging round with, and me included, were the worser end of the social scale of travellers. We weren't a movement, just a bunch of pissed-up people, some so nasty not even I would talk to them. For me it was a lot to do with drinking. I didn't really know it but I was an alcoholic. I drank a hell of a lot. The whole thing was very self-destructive.

When I look back on it it's quite sad really because a lot of us had really positive ideas and we thought we were doing something really worthwhile and important, but all we were doing really was killing ourselves. We convinced ourselves that everything was against us but the truth was we were probably our own worst enemies. Best leave that to the psychologists. But you can't handle that sort of life for long. Most of the people I know from then have stopped or cut down a lot.

Sitting on a street corner drinking brew all day isn't a positive thing to do, but I wouldn't knock people for doing it because I've done it myself. I can understand that attitude: 'God, this world is a shithole, I'm so small, it's so big, what can I do? I'll just get pissed and forget about it.' It is very head-in-the-sand, and part of the whole traveller thing is about running away from society, but then that's understandable – there's a lot of bad things to be running away from. For me and people like me it was the sort of end of the line really. And for a lot of the people starting out now it's the same. For others the appeal is quite romantic. It's the English dream really, isn't it? – the fantasy most English people have: trees, fields, all those images from *Tess of the D'Urbervilles*. People accuse the band of being romantic like that but we're not, we're a lot more realistic than that. I just like the freedom, seeing all my friends. I knew when I went to a festival that there would be thousands of people similar enough to me that I'd feel secure. I never felt secure in life in general, still don't in many ways, but being with other travellers at festivals is when I've felt most comfortable. I'll probably be back out there when all this band business has finished.

I suppose as a group we made a conscious decision to distance ourselves from the travellers' thing, really just to widen our audience. For us the festivals were places to play when no one else would have us. After a while though there's no point in just playing to the same people – any group wants to be heard as widely as possible. But now we've done that we've still kept a lot of the original people who liked us. We always get accused of selling-out and all that, we got accused of being sell-outs when we made a record, like that was some kind of betrayal. But that's just a minority really. We play big venues now and a lot can't afford to come and see us, but some blag their way in and they're always welcome to do that.

We never play small festivals now and haven't done for a couple of years, they'd just become Levellers gigs and that would ruin what the festival's about really. We still get labelled with it though and get a lot of stick for it. Some bloke sent us a letter saying, 'Dear Hippie Parasites, why should I work forty-five hours a week and pay £500 a month mortgage so you lot can wander round with dogs on strings smoking roll-ups and drinking cider? I would napalm you and your followers. Get a life, get washed, grow up and start listening to The Fall, you social inadequates.' He put his name and address and phone number on it so we printed the whole thing in the fan club magazine for a laugh. I'd love to hear all the phone calls he gets.

You might as well do things like that. I wrote a letter to Peter Lilley, the secretary of state for social security, about his plans for cutting benefits for travellers. He was cutting it for other people as well, people with HIV, women in refuge hostels, but travellers mainly, because they're the easiest to attack. It's hard to get a job when you haven't got an address but after the media hate campaign of the summer he knows he can cut that with full public approval, whereas he knows if he cuts more hospitals people aren't going to stand for it. I just made a few points – about what it would cost to rehouse everyone, especially when there's a massive homeless problem and even people in regular jobs are getting evicted because they can't pay their mortgages; about the problems the police would have forcing a massive amount of people off the road against their will. It was a very restrained, quite well thought out, letter. He won't take any notice of course but you've got to make an effort.

I suppose it was inevitable that one of those festival bands would break through and we were just lucky it was us. It could have been any of us really – RDF, Culture Shock, Chumbawumba, Ozric Tentacles. Culture Shock aren't going any more but I think if they were still around they're the ones who would be in the position we're in now – it was really happening for them before they split up. And there's a few good bands that actually live on the road and do all the festivals like Poisoned Electrichead and 2000 DS.

In some ways the festivals were more fun than what we do now as a band but in some ways not. I don't miss wading through a load of mud to get on stage. Drinking a lot helps with all that discomfort side of things and I don't drink at all now. I look back on them with great fondness and I still consider myself part of it – I've still got the same friends and I still do the festivals. It's quite nice now doing them without having to play. People moan at me for not playing, though. When we did Glastonbury last year I was staying on the travellers' site about six miles away before I had to go on the main official site to play and people were coming up and saying, 'If you don't play on the travellers' site you're bastards.' We'd planned to play there, there was us and RDF and Back to the Planet that were going to do it but the site got evicted and moved somewhere else and none of us could find it. There wasn't really very good facilities to play a gig anyway.

Festivals have changed a bit and had a lot more attention because of the rave business. When that first happened I thought it was really good, bringing in a lot of straight people who were getting into the travellers' life and maybe opening their minds a bit. I remember walking around Reading three years ago and seeing my first rave/ hippie convoy type crossover and thinking that was really happening. But the friction between the ravers and travellers has ruined things a bit. For them it's a night's anarchy then you go home; for the travellers they have to live there and suffer the consequences.

But no one knows who really causes the mess and the trouble. There's a lot of shit travellers about – more now than there ever has been – and it's just convenient to blame it all on the ravers. I'm just bored of the music. Because I don't do any drugs like that, the music just means nothing to me. I'm not very good at staying up late either. I'm a bit boring really.

I'd still be out there now though if it wasn't for the band. It's the only place I've felt really comfortable. It's quite unfortunate for me in a way that the band's got so big. Even at festival sites and that you get looked at strangely. People never used to care in the past.

And I don't really like living in a house much. It's fucking cold. People say, 'Oh you're moving in to keep warm in the winter', but all we've got in there is a poxy little gas fire and you have to keep feeding the meter with 50p pieces all the time. The burner in my truck's about ten times as warm.

MARK

In the summer of 1991, the old hippie festivals began to mutate into venues for rave music. Many older travellers still view the ravers with suspicion. They hate the noise, and many hate the new synthetic drugs like ecstasy and the flashy dealers who sell them. But most of all they hate the attention raves bring. By 1992 the numbers of ravers attending them had helped swell the festivals to a size not seen since before the Beanfield in 1985.

Festival raves grew out of the warehouse parties and illegal raves of the late eighties. Spiral Tribe were among the first, and are still the most famous, of all the sound systems that brought raves to festivals during the summer of 1991, but there are others, like Bedlam, Circus Warp, Circus Normal and Circus Irritant. The sound systems aren't formal organisations, just loose affiliations of people, but the parties they put on are highly organised. Would-be ravers learn of a phone number days before an event, through fliers, word of mouth or by listening to pirate radio. In the hours before an event the phone will give out clues to the location so that crowds gather in the general area. When the site is taken, the exact location goes out. The idea is that by the time the police find out what's going on, the site will have too many people on it for the police to be able to shift them.

Thirteen of Spiral Tribe's members were arrested after the free festival at Castlemorton Common in 1992, when upwards of twenty thousand people attended an eight-day event.

Mark was one of those arrested. He's in his thirties, a charismatic, good-looking man, who is one of the central core of Spiral Tribe, and one of their main ideologues, disseminating the strangely mystical Spiral creed. He is intense, but smiles almost *constantly while he talks. He's living in a large house in West Hampstead owned by one of the members. The basement has a recording studio, turning out techno tapes most hours of the day. Their next-door neighbour has complained to the environmental health department.*

Spiral Tribe T-shirts, featuring spiral motifs and their mystical number '23' were popular on sites in the summer of 1992. Since Castlemorton, Spiral Tribe now have a record contract with the Big Life label. They were signed up by Jazz Summers, who once managed Wham!

I t's spiral. It has no beginning, but the major day was probably the day we took the sound system out of London, where we were doing warehouse parties, to go to the festivals. It wasn't a conscious decision, decisions are not part of this process. The moment is ever manifesting.

The first we went to was the summer solstice in 1991, which in this day and age is not at Stonehenge, but as close as you can get. That year it was down at Longstock. I was a sceptical soul up until that point, but something happened to me there that's never happened before. The pennies dropped. I haven't felt energy like it. We were totally enchanted by the whole thing. As a sound system we walked out the front door and we haven't come back yet.

The police were there in force of course and the helicopters were hovering overhead. A dramatic stage was set. The weekend after that we went to the next festival, and then the next festival . . . That summer we went out it was non-stop. The weekends overlapped into weeks.

In those days we just had a Luton box van which didn't work very well. We'd pack it up with the sound system and then borrow somebody's AA or RAC card and phone them up. This helped us to get into sites that were blocked by the police, as well as out of them. Sound system relayed out of the area!

There are a few people who moan and they do moan very loudly and they whine and they whinge. Maybe they have a point from their own personal point of view but as far as we know, free festivals are about playing music non-stop. Techno is folk music. Never before has folk music been so accessible or so loud. It's always been down to the tin whistles or whatever.

There was a guy there, at that first solstice, who came up on Sunday morning asking us to turn the music down. These people may have been travelling for years, but we've just come through hell and high water to bring them this sound system for nothing, and to keep it going. In that situation we're very polite about it, but no fucking way. There's been so many people trying to hold this thing together for so long and we would never be there in the first place if we weren't there by popular demand. We play the people's music.

The music has an amazing effect karmically on each and every person who comes into contact with it. It goes into the realms of shamanism. You can call us techno-pagans, whatever, but these are very fundamental energies. Spiral Tribe are a concept that is trying to de-label itself by being the Spiral Tribe, everybody, everything, interconnecting. Now is a great time. Technology has speeded up quite incredibly, but also, it's coupled with a global process of self-realisation.

There was no real divide between us and the older travellers until Castlemorton. It was a thing made by the press. It was only after Castlemorton, after the arrests and prosecutions of Spiral Tribe, that we began to witness any story in the press that there was any kind of difference between ravers and travellers. Up till then things were going very nicely.

We left Castlemorton on the Friday and got ambushed by the police. The guys say, 'We are just doing our job,' and it takes you a while to realise that they are telling the truth. They are the soldier ants on the anthill of the establishment. They confiscated all our vehicles, in all about seven or eight of them, so it left us without homes, without our sound systems and without our lights.

They had us in cells overnight then up in court the next day before they released us on the most stringent bail conditions. We had to report to our home address three times a week, no matter where that was. Then we were thrown out into this pouring rain, no money, no means of transport, no clothes. We camped out on the police station door almost two weeks, much to their embarrassment. It escalated the whole situation into a protest about the whole thing, and the local community brought down tarpaulins and sleeping bags. This wasn't just the hardcore geezers, there were kids there and families.

The police are holding us responsible for Castlemorton. Seven of us have got to go to court in two months on a charge of causing a public nuisance. We prefer to call it causing a public new sense. I know that some of our critics accuse us of bringing it on top and allowing the government to bring in legislation that they wouldn't have bothered with beforehand, but this is a catalyst. There are great injustices and great wrongs and we are standing up and being counted. Apparently the sentences could be heavy. We don't know. I could turn up there and be locked up for a couple of years. The way we see this, any kind of negative polarity is going to generate its own positive.

Castlemorton we were going six days non-stop. Camelford in August '91 we were going fourteen days, twenty-four hours. To experience that you experience a world you didn't know existed. The sun goes down, the moon comes up and you see the world spinning. My record is nine days without sleep. It's a shamanic thing.

Anyone comes down there and asks us to turn it down, I'm sorry, we're not going to. Turn it up if anything. If you've got a voice, shout. Our attitude is, 'Make some fucking noise.'

SIMON

The members of the Bedlam sound system started setting up at festivals early in the summer of 1992. It's a looser, more relaxed set-up than Spiral Tribe. Simon Goose has been helping to organise parties for them since he came off remand at the beginning of that year.

For the winter he's moved into a squat in Hackney. He has one child by an earlier relationship, and his girlfriend is pregnant. He is sitting in the basement playing a game of Risk with Adam, one of the people he shares the squat with. Adam's holed up in Siberia. Simon has taken over the entire New World. 'Peru,' he says, 'good cocaine.' Dogs snuffle round the table, occasionally threatening to upset all the pieces. The table is littered with cigarette papers and bits of torn-up card.

Simon has lots of old tattoos. On one upper arm there's a coloured-in picture of a skinhead in DMs. There are large scars from where he removed the words 'England' and 'National Front'. As a teenager he was a member of the Young National Front, and used to do security for skin gigs. His girlfriend is black. 'She knows about all that,' he says. 'It's another chapter.'

I first started going to all the raves around Biggin Hill in 1988. I was well into it. I used to be on the commercial side of raving until about eighteen months ago. I don't know why I stopped. I caught the vibe a bit. It's more than just like a party or a way of earning money, there's a whole social scene that goes with it. You get an average party, if there's 800 people there, you know 200 of them as friends you can have a laugh with. That takes over from money.

We don't charge any more. I'd rather dress up as a clown and run round with the bucket. We're not a big organisation of drug dealers. Some systems are, that's how they can remain free, but we're not into that. We respect our freedom now, especially me more than others.

I'm a city boy but during the summer you get that vibe to get out of London. Bedlam was the second biggest sound system at Castlemorton, plus our lot found the site. Don't you believe what you read in the papers about Spiral Tribe finding it. They were the last system there.

We'd been to Lechlade, played there, done a party in Stroud, went and chilled out in Wales for a bit and then went looking for the Avon Free Festival. We knew it was going to be one of the biggest things England had seen for a long time. We were in the spastic bus, a converted disabled ambulance, and we had a Panorama coach, a fire engine and two small buses.

I saw the site at Castlemorton before there were any buses on it. I just beat a five-mile convoy into the place and I watched it come in. It's a buzz. There are bigger buzzes in your life than just drugs. You can get out of your face but there's a natural buzz when you watch a place fill up like that. You can't do nothing but smile, pulling that off and watching the police just standing by. There was nothing they could do.

I was there for the full week. There's so many people that you know, you just wander round, lunching out in everyone's buses. You have a dance if you like, go and check out the generators, check out the DJs. We finally turned the music off Monday night because we could tell everyone was getting jarred with loud music. Not just the local people who lived in Castlemorton, but the people who lived on site started to get annoyed too. There was almost a big punch-up when Spirals refused to turn the music off. 'We're hardcore,' and all that attitude.

In a group like Bedlam if there's twenty or thirty involved with you then it's not a lot of work. At one point we had all the rigs on buses so anywhere we went we could steam in, drop it all out, plug it in and we've got a party. All you need is an empty warehouse and a pair of bolt-cutters. We used to have mobile phones. At eight o'clock in the evening the phones would start ringing: 'Where's the party? Where's the party?' Call back later. You give them a couple of clues. Then about eleven, twelve, you've got everything set up, they call back . . . People say that parties are just drug supermarkets. Yeah, people take drugs. Of course they take drugs, that's why they go to parties. But if you go to one square mile of any major city and take out all the drugs from those houses there will be no difference in quantity. The only difference is that it's people in buses with drugs instead of rich little wise kids from the city.

Drugs only became illegal because the poor people got them. It was all very fashionable in the eighteenth century to sit back and smoke opium. Even royalty was smoking opium and taking cocaine in those days. It wouldn't be too surprising if royalty was smoking dope these days. All the kids of earls and dukes, they're still getting hooked on heroin, but it's OK for them, they're rich, it's not a social problem.

Four years ago I was in a right mess from heroin and crack, running around like a total lunatic. All my morals have completely switched. I hate people who come to parties coked out of their heads with real attitude, 'Mmm, I take coke!' And if I catch people with syringes I want to shove them up their arses. I was a cunt back then, pure and simple.

I was a gun-toting crackhead. I know the people who are carrying guns now and I cunt them off to their face. They say, 'But such and such could happen.' It ain't going to happen and if it does it's because you've got that inside your jacket.

I'm really an anti-violence person now. I remember going to Ziggy's in Streatham in '89 and seeing someone get shot. It was one of the most horrific things I've ever seen in my life. There was no talking or anything, all you heard was a bang and an explosion of blood. I was actually looking in the direction it happened in. I've seen people stabbed before and there's lots and lots of blood. When someone's shot there's an explosion of blood. This one got shot in the arse and there was loads of it. It was nasty. We just ran out of the club. We didn't want to be there. I don't know if he made it.

I've been stabbed at the football. That was all part of the gun-toting crackhead days. We used to think it would be a laugh to go and get really cracked out of our head and go to a football match and have a ruck. They were quite amusing days those . . .

I'm from South London. At school I thought I was Jack the Peanut. At a later stage they figured out I had dyslexia and that's half the reason I couldn't sit still in a classroom. I was sent off to a special school as a boarder, Whitstone Head near Bude in Cornwall. I was there for a year and all they did was open my eyes to glue-sniffing, sex and hash. I used to run away and turn up at the traveller sites down there. 'Oh yeah, cute little runaway.'

I carried on getting into trouble and got put into a detention centre when I was fourteen. Between fourteen and nineteen I'd done five custodials and three remands, most of them for minor offences like petty burglary. The most serious was a street robbery. After I came out I thought, 'Well, you're nineteen now, you've been pratting about for the last few years of your life, it's about time you settled down and sorted your life out.'

I managed it for a couple of years. Went and did a City and Guilds in bricklaying. Very good timing. What happens? The recession happens. No work about unless you're really fast at bricklaying. It got to the point where it wasn't even worth looking for a job so I started going partying at weekends, sat in bed till Thursday, then started partying again. And then, no money, can't go partying, oh fuck, better go and cause some crime.

I moved in with this girl and we were spending like a grand a week on cocaine and smack. You have to do plenty of crime for that. What I got nicked for was for doing burglaries, but I was doing loads of other things. I was on remand for six months with this guy, and after six months I was thinking, 'Yeah, get back out there, carry on being a bad boy.'

I got the sentence and it worked out that I had to do another four months, and during that four months I got caught trying to help a mate escape, so they gave me a bit more. It came to an eighteen-month stretch altogether. During that time I was in my cell getting information about the people I used to hang round with. There was a couple of murders. The mate I was in court with before got stabbed thirty-four times and one geezer got found in a shallow grave in Tatsfield. Another guy chopped up another geezer with a machete. It was quite a weird scene. I can't go into it too deep, but people are serving time for it all.

I thought to myself, 'This is full of shit. When you get out, don't have it with any of them.' I haven't been back to Croydon since. If I did I'd probably end up as a fucked-up mess in six months.

I went back in a little while back for burglary, three months on remand. I nicked someone's Five Series, plus I tried to nick their Audi Sport. My co-defendant admitted to everything because he knew he was in the shit for sure. So when I came up to court the jury found me not guilty. Not guilty!

If you know what you're doing in gaol you can have a fucking laugh. When I was in remand in Oxford that last time I had people that were going out on releases once a week and bringing me four ounces of hash. I was going out on visits on Sundays and handing out three or four hundred quid I'd made. In Oxford they had this big thing about me making too much money in there and they knew it.

Top three subjects when you're stuck in a cell: puff, women and sitting at home and watching TV. Simple things are the ones you miss. You think about going into a shop and buying a packet of fags. And you think, 'This is a waste of time.'

Like I say, if we find people with syringes now we chuck them out. We don't want that vibe in our party. I do a bit of coke now and again but it's more of a treat. I do it for a laugh, it's not that I'll cane this and then go and get loads more. I've got control of it. I had some at the weekend and it's the first I've had any since that eighteen-month sentence.

We're trying to buy a bus at the moment. You can buy a decent Panorama for about £800 to a grand, but we want to have a bit of money to spend on it and do it up because there will be a few of us living on it. It's like a little family. We hate each other, slag each other off, but we've known each other a long time.

Four years ago I looked really respectable. I had a Renault Five Turbo, all the clothes and the money, but I was a real shit. Now I look like a real crustie cunt. It's a whole new chapter, a whole new lifestyle.

If you want to call us 'travellers' you can, but we're a new breed. Most of us have come from the slums of the cities. We're different from them. They sit there admiring their crystal and we'll sit there admiring our vinyl, know what I mean? There have been hippies going for years and years, but they've all stagnated, especially after the Bean-field. Everyone buggered off after that. No one dared bring a sound system into a field and just play up for days and days. Sound systems have brought the travellers back. The anti-rave cosmic hippies sit there and moan and groan about rave music, but people had forgotten the travellers existed until now.

That's one of the reasons they don't like it.

JADE

*Jade is getting into healing. It's about feeling energy. She's living
at a friend's house after spending the summer as a traveller with
Spiral Tribe and Bedlam. Also living in the house is a bull terrier
called Spoon who is ill. His throat is half-paralysed after an
accident and he has trouble eating. Jade has been healing Spoon.
She puts her hands over the dog's neck and concentrates on
passing the good energy from one hand and drawing the negative
energy from the other. 'You've got to feel the heat going through,'
she says.*

*Jade has close-cropped hair and a ring through her nose. Last
year she dropped out of college.*

I started taking ecstasy in September '91, and before that
I was just at poly in Oxford doing occupational ther-
apy. I used to be into all the disco music, and I was doing
quite well at college. I quit in December in my second
year.

That time, a year ago, I had just a couple of rings in my
ears, not all the ones I have now, and I had no ring
through my nose then either. And I had dark curly hair in
ringlets down to my shoulders. At a festival in July '92 I
shaved the sides off and left a long bit on top, then I
shaved the back off as well, so I just had one long tuft, and
finally about a month ago I took the rest off.

When you take your hair off it changes how you feel
because you know that whatever anyone's looking at, it's
just you. You haven't got hair in your face hiding you. So

you can concentrate on other things. It's a really nice feeling.

In my third term at poly I went out on placement. That's when I started smoking hash. I started realising that it was quite a chilled-out way of life. But I just used to be really boring, go to the pub every night, come back, crash out at eleven. In the last year everything has changed. I don't look at drugs as bad now. Drugs don't mess up your head, people mess up your head. As long as you know when to stop, when you've had enough, then you're all right. But I would never have changed if it hadn't been for acid. I took my first trip in January and in about February, March, I actually started thinking.

My first acid trip was New Year's Eve '91. I was at a club called Fantasia, it was like a £25 ticket deal but I got in free, and it was like a total party trip. I got off my head just laughing, giggling, saying, 'Oh, look at that, look at that.' Nothing more than just a visual experience, I didn't use my mind. My next trip I actually started thinking, just imagining what would happen if everybody in the world put all their energy together. I was imagining it from a satellite's point of view, thinking about what on earth it would look like if everybody concentrated on having flames coming out of their hands at night.

That spring I went to a rave in a warehouse in Acton. It was advertised on a flier. I thought that Spiral Tribe and Bedlam and all the names on the piece of paper were just another rave set-up. I didn't know they were anything more.

Then on May Day Bank Holiday I went to Lechlade, Gloucester, which was my first free festival party. I was just like, wow. There were ten thousand people there. I didn't know anything could be quite like it. That's where I met up with Spiral Tribe. Wow. It was just excellent. It was light when I arrived, so it must have been in the morning. First thing I saw was the police, of course, standing on the outside wasting their time, and loads of people dancing, loads of travellers' vehicles. What a weekend. I arrived Saturday and left Wednesday night.

When you weren't dancing you could go and hang around with all the people who were sitting round campfires or sitting by the lake that was there and just deal with people. It was wicked.

The following week I went to a rave in Stroud and I met Mitch, this geezer from Spiral Tribe who lived in a caravan. I knew there was no turning back, really. I can remember thinking, 'Yeah, it's got to be now.' The next week I spent just sorting out what I had to sort out. I did a load of shopping, got a mattress and put it in the back of my red Ford Escort estate and then I gave Mitch a lift up to Wales the next week where he was going to join up with some people from Spiral Tribe. I just went to Wales and never went home. At Lechlade when I'd seen the travellers I thought, 'I really couldn't live like that,' but two weeks later I just decided to go on the road. Because it was time to move on from Oxford, so I went and totally messed up my head in one big bang and got it sorted out.

That's how I ended up staying with the Spirals in Wales. I didn't know what to make of it, because I didn't really know any of them. I was just stuck in the mountains with these people I hadn't really met.

But we went from Wales to Castlemorton Common, and after that everything just went *whoosh*. The festival at Castlemorton was mind-blowing, because I'd never been anywhere where there had been twenty-five thousand people before. I thought it was wicked but I didn't know much different because it was only my second festival.

The rigs were playing all the time, lots of different sound systems, there was so much going on, loads and loads of food for sale. You'd basically walk about buying food when you're hungry, hang around for a while, do some dancing. It seemed like the five days was just one day, because you don't have night and day at something like that, you just sleep when you're tired. I don't know how much sleep I got.

There was only a little bit of violence. There was some quite crap stuff, like one geezer getting the windows of his car smashed for driving thirty miles an hour through the site where there were kids. Probably people on Special Brew. Fair play, if you think what would have happened if he'd run over some kid. But I don't think hitting someone's window is right. You just tell them to slow down.

I don't think anyone realised how many people were there until afterwards. I remember someone got hold of a newspaper which had a story about it and a few people had tvs, but it seemed that the locals were really friendly, smiling and happy, driving past, and then we heard that all this stuff was going on saying the locals *weren't* happy. I was thinking, 'Who?' The locals who had been anywhere near the site realised that it wasn't as bad as it seemed. It was just the fear of what the media were saying about it.

I was lucky. I left Castlemorton early, so I didn't get my car pulled by the police. The rest of the Spirals got everything impounded. After Castlemorton, they didn't have any vehicles except for one Transit. After that we spent the week sleeping outside Worcester police station which was really, really excellent. We had absolutely nothing . . . nothing at all. We got given plastic sheets to put over us because it was raining, and people came down and gave us food, bread, blankets, and the locals came out and gave us bedding. It turned out to be a really good week. And the press came down. And because there seemed to be more Spirals there, because they seemed to have had the most vehicles impounded, it made me think, 'Yeah, Spirals, really wicked.'

I went back and stayed on site in Watford with Spiral Tribe for four months. We had one lorry or one massive bender that we all slept in on site, or out on a sofa next to the fire. Everyone sleeps anywhere.

When you first get into it, it's like, 'Oh, man, I've found the people I want to be with.' But after a while you realise they're not as sorted as they seem. I just spent the summer trying to work them out. They just seemed to be ego. There is no loving and caring, it's just sheer anarchy. I came to the conclusion that they were messing up my head and I didn't want to be with them at all. Spirals are a bit chauvinistic. There aren't many women involved, they've got a male ego. They seem to think that women are softcore and you've got to be hardcore.

So I moved. In September I went to live with Bedlam on a site in Petersfield, which was wicked fun. Bedlam is a group of people with a sound system that put free parties on at the weekend. Bedlam aren't as close-knit as Spiral Tribe. Spiral Tribe are all together in one little group, and they work together. Bedlam is more a weekend thing. People go to sites or to squats and come back together for parties. There's no, 'You should be doing this.' There was a cottage on site and people who didn't have vehicles could live there. Now I'm back in London looking for a squat.

When I think back, I was just so, so, so straight. My parents live in Slough. I went to an all girls' boarding-school called Woldingham near Caterham in Surrey from the age of eleven to the age of eighteen. It was right in the middle of a beautiful valley and had a two-mile drive either side. You weren't allowed out in the evenings, you weren't allowed out at weekends, you weren't allowed out on Sundays. Basically, all you could do was go shopping on a Saturday afternoon. If you wanted to you could go home for the weekend, which my parents didn't want me to do, 'cos I lived so far away.

I can't blame them for it because I did have a choice. You either go to day-school which is going to be crap and horrible and rubbish, or you go to boarding-school and it's going to be wicked. So I said, 'I'll go to boarding-school.' I don't know. I'm quite grateful for the way I've been brought up. All I've ever had is love, so I'm quite lucky. But I had such a sheltered life. When I was eighteen I still didn't know how to approach a bloke.

My dad's a chartered accountant, my mum's a house-wife, if you can call it that, because she's got a maid who comes in and does all the housework. I think that's disgusting, to be honest, having little slaves to do all your dirty work, it makes me feel sick. But, they're happy the way they are, so leave them to it. They're Catholic, very conservative, just a typical upper-class family. Their lives revolve around money. Mum is into lovely clothes and her cars.

I'm off to India for two months soon, Delhi, Rajasthan, everywhere, with a mate who's been before. We were going to be going a month ago but we lunched out all the money. I'm madly in love with this geezer, and he's got a girlfriend and he's decided he doesn't want a girlfriend at all and that's it basically. So it's, 'Oh God! I'm off. See you later.'

I just know that I'm going to see things that I haven't seen before. I know I'm going to see poverty and healing and a lot of meditation. If you go with the headspace that you're paranoid, then you just mash your head up, but if you go to learn things then you know you're going to have a really positive time at the end of it. There's nothing to be scared of.

I know I'm going to come back totally different. I'm going to come back sorted. When I come back from India I really would like to get a vehicle together. And I really want to travel.

I think if I can change from being totally straight, then anyone can. Society is such a mess that I have no intention of going back into it the way it is.

PART FIVE

THE FOUR-WHEELED FAMILY

HARRY

The Gypsy Liaison Officer drives up the hill to where he has heard some 'new age travellers' are squatting on a council gravel tip. He's a large man, ex-army. When he took the job, over six years ago now, there was a clause in his contract that told him that he should expect both verbal and physical abuse. 'All that came true,' he remembers.

The county he works for has a policy of asking all travellers squatting council land to register for fixed sites under the 1968 Caravan Sites Act. It may sound like eagerness to provide homes for them, but in fact it is one of the many aspects of bureaucratic fencing the travellers find themselves taking part in. The GLO will drive up to a site and hand over a pro forma questionnaire in which they are invited to apply for a permanent site. But the county council know that to complete the forms they will have to give their full names, so it is unlikely that any traveller will fill it in. The moment their names are known they can be prosecuted for damage done to a site while they are squatting. By refusing to fill in the form they also release the council from any obligation under the '68 Act to look after them, leaving it clear for the council to evict them.

The Liaison Officer sees all sorts. He's had people living in holes in the ground, people living up trees, people living under bits of canvas. He's seen people covered in mud and filth which he still finds hard to cope with. He was a soldier for twenty-six years. He says it's easy to keep clean, even outdoors. Once he came across a baby in a box outside a caravan being looked after by a dog. The bitch had a litter of her own, and was licking the baby. He went inside the caravan and told the mother he'd have to report her to social services. Later he drove to Mothercare and bought things for her with his own money. The scene distressed him a great deal, though he sometimes wonders whether he would have batted an eyelid if it had been a child in a back garden of a house with the family pet.

Then there are the local residents, and the farmers whose land is being squatted. Last night he was at a meeting, listening to a farmer who said he had had fifteen sheep mauled to death by travellers' dogs and eleven more which needed the vet.

The GLO believes that you can't just wipe out the travellers; they won't just go away. He has photographs in his office of gypsies in the 1890s. Sometimes he looks at them and thinks how much they look like the kids he sees living in benders and shelters now.

The GLO drives up to the gravel tip on the B3170, just up the hill from Corfe Castle. He knocks on the door of the largest vehicle, a big Leyland truck. The back door opens and a large snarling Dobermann springs out, dragging a couple of young women behind it. 'Stand back,' one shouts. 'It might go for you.' The GLO has been bitten several times in the course of duty, so he doesn't take any chances. He retreats hastily off the site.

When the dog has been chained up, the GLO leans his briefcase against a Mini on the site, fishes out a few of the pro forma questionnaires and hands them to the two girls and their mother. A goat, half-Angora, strolls up casually and starts chewing the sheets of paper. The women laugh.

Back at county hall that afternoon he tells the others in the office, 'I've almost had the arse bitten out of my trousers.'

The Dobermann belongs to Hazel. She's twenty-two and has been a traveller all her life. She was in her mother Harry's truck when she saw the GLO come on to the layby where they're parked up.

Harry is forty-four, but looks much younger. Her other two daughters are also in the truck: Plum, who is nineteen, and Frances, her youngest, who is eight. Hazel drove down in her truck yesterday from Kent where she spent the autumn picking apples and hops. She is visiting for a few days on her way to Cornwall to pick daffodils. She's a trained horsebreaker.

Plum has a caravan she pulls round with an Austin Princess. She didn't go to school much, but after O-levels she enrolled at college to do an engineering course. She passed.

Last night, after Hazel had turned up, they all went to the pub because they hadn't seen each other for a while. Today they're all clutching their heads.

Sometimes, when they're there drinking tea and giggling at each other's stories, calling each other names, talking about all the stupid things they've done together, they're like a family from a children's book who ran away to the circus.

As the evening wears on, Plum lights the paraffin lamps. At the front of the truck there's a bunk bed. The burner stands by the door at the back. Soon it warms up and Harry has to open the top half of the door to let in the night air. Next to the bed are the forms the Gypsy Liaison Officer has left. They'll make something for Frances to draw on.

Harry rolls a cigarette and says, 'The Gypsy Liaison Officer took us for a bunch of idiots. We know what bits of paper they need and how long we can stay on a place and who owns it.'

Plum is sitting on a cushion next to her mother. 'They try all sorts of things,' she grins. 'Like they get a sheet of A4 paper, type a few words on it and hand it to you and say, "Get off, you've got a week." They think you'll go, "Oh dear. Got to go." ' Both daughters share their mother's Yorkshire accent.

'Sometimes they'll come on and say, "Who's the man in charge?" ' says Harry. 'Who's in charge? I don't know. It's a family. No one's in charge. We send out Frances when they say that,' they laugh. Frances looks up from her drawing. Oddly enough, she's drawing a picture of a house: four windows and a front door. 'They seem to think you can't do anything without a mastermind in charge. You couldn't do anything off your own bat.'

'In Hampshire,' remembers Plum, 'there was a load of us sat in a truck and these officials all came up and said, "Can we speak to the menfolk." And we said, "We are the menfolk. We just dressed ourselves up as women." And we were going, "Oh ho ho ho," in deep manly voices and slapping our thighs and pulling our trousers down so you could see the top of our bums. Saying to each other, "Come here, wench." And they just went off because

we were being so daft. Speak to the menfolk? What are they on about?'

'Anyway,' says Harry, 'I reckon they'll give us a month, but we won't be here by the time they come to evict us. We'd planned on coming to Cornwall to do the daffodils for Christmas, but we don't want to tell him. We want him to waste his time,' she laughs.

I've been travelling about twenty years. Plum and Hazel have been travelling since they were born.

I tried putting Hazel into school when she was five but she didn't stay long. They had her stood in the corner and everything. It was chaos. She was already reading books, halfway through reading *Lord of the Rings* and they were like 'C-A- T', 'J-A-N-E'. They said she had to do that too because she was in that class because of her age, rather than finding something that suited her ability. So she got really naughty and started giggling and throwing things and disrupting other kids. And there were weird things about religion and God too. She came home singing funny hymns. 'Jesus' hands are kind hands'; 'Give me joy in my heart, Give me Jesus'. I would think, 'What's she singing *that* for?' So we took her out.

There's about three years between Hazel and Plum. By the time Plum was about to start we could see that school had nothing to offer them, so she never started. They were both deregistered with local authorities. The point is that the educational standards are so low in this country that it's so easy for a five-year-old to be able to pass their tests. It's ridiculous. Later on we had some welfare officer come round to check on them with some work he considered a ten-year-old and an eight-year-old should be able to do. They passed OK.

I didn't really have any major plans about teaching them, just that I was going to leave God out of it really. Completely out of it. I decided that I wasn't going to teach them anything before they were nine or ten unless they asked me to. None of this making them sit down and do funny handwriting, none of that stuff. I used to read to them, and talk to them about whatever was going on. It just went from there.

When we went to France they went to school for about six months in a French grammar in Bordeaux. That was a lot better than the English schools, they were more open.

Hazel went to college which she found hard. The discipline there was hard for her to understand. Society sees that sort of obedience as having respect for your teachers but it's not. What it is is a lack of respect for the students. Respect should be mutual. You have to learn to think for yourself. They can't teach you what your moral and social ethics should be. All you need to teach children is how to get information.

The one big problem on the road is that a lot of the time there aren't any children. Frances is eight. Finding her someone to play with is nearly impossible. Every few months we happen to see a child for a few days and she has someone to play with. There's a lot of babies and a few teenagers but there aren't actually many families with children that you can go and call for.

But I think life on the road is a better upbringing for children than school. Myself, I went to a convent, which explains it all really, doesn't it? I used to get caned for giggling. How can you get caned for doing something like that? It was a really serious crime. I was kicked out when I was about fourteen, for sliding down the banisters. Fancy being kicked out of school for something like that.

I think the idea of travelling was always there. It was a big family. When we were little kids we used to build dens and sleep in tents in the garden and leave home for long missions with water containers and stuff. Where I grew up we had a big wood at the back of the garden. As children, in the summers, we lived underneath this bender we built in the woods, and we used to build treehouses and my mum used to take us sandwiches.

My mother was like an eccentric artist, she used to paint and do mad things, and she was a Catholic too. We all blame it on our mother. She never minded about me becoming a traveller at all. In fact when my brother

Bernard got his bus she sewed him all the curtains because she was a seamstress, and my dad built cupboards in it for him too. I had four brothers. The lads used to mend motorbikes in the sink. Some of them are on the road now still: I've got a brother in France.

I had a dodgy marriage in the beginning, so I left home in Yorkshire. I went and got on the Magic Bus, a cheap bus company for people on the hippie trail. It was '71, '72 and I'd just had Hazel. She and I went to Turkey first, to Istanbul which was good fun. And then I found that I had spent all my money and I didn't have enough to get back on, and ended up selling my return ticket and my shoes. I got a bit hungry, but it was meant to be like that – *enlightenment* and stuff. I waited in Istanbul for my brother to send me some money in the post and while we waited we begged for a while and sat around. Eventually we met this Turkish family who had this place in the hills. The husband used to come down into Istanbul and do their shopping for his wife. One day he said, 'I've got a shed if you want it.' So we went and stayed in this shed and helped his wife out because she had about eleven kids and was pregnant again. We did that for a while, and it was really good getting out into the Turkish community. I got into the local drink and into generally going, '*Yah-hoo!*'

I've got a twin brother, and he arrived out in Istanbul too. At the time he was a student so he was really into it. Back then we were both devotees of Guru Maharaji, getting into meditation. We came back but I couldn't settle down after that. After Istanbul we went back to live in Leeds and actually opened our own ashram in Chapeltown. It lasted quite a while that phase, before we decided it was just as much of a load of rubbish as Catholicism. My twin brother went to Bradford Art College and I trailed off again.

I started off working for another brother who had a hotel. Then I went off trailing round Blackpool and Morecombe and all that coast, working in and out of hotels, doing chambermaiding, sometimes staying in the hotels, sometimes staying in caravans. I had Plum too then.

I did have a go at settling down. What happened was
we bought a guest-house in Harrogate and I did it up and
we began running that. I bought it quite cheap. I'm quite
good at making money. It was a lovely house, we were
posh then, and I gave it my best shot, about three years,
but it was horrible. I hated it. For one thing, I found that I
was drinking all the time because I couldn't cope with it,
and we were not together, losing communication, working all the time, acquiring things we didn't even want,
you know, always buying *towels*. It was horrible. I would
stop and think, 'What am I doing all this for? What is at
the end of it? You're getting old.' So we just got rid of it,
sold it.

With the money, we went to France, and spent it all
having really good fun. We spent every penny. What we
did was go and stay in really posh hotels, jet-setting up
and down the Côte d'Azur, lived in Cannes in a big hotel,
and bought lovely clothes and jewellery. There were
some really fancy hotels with movie stars and pop stars,
hotels where you got a table with, like, eight waiters
trying to pass you a fork so you could eat your dinner.

Hazel was about nine or ten, Plum was seven. We did
all sorts of stupid things, like doing our washing in the
hotel swimming pool. At one place we stayed in this really
posh room and cooked in there. We spilt ravioli all over
this really expensive carpet, and upset the wine all over
the Axminster. They didn't say anything.

One hotel we stayed at, it turned up that Elton John was
there too. Plum and Hazel were scrabbling round trying
to get a look at his hair to see if it was a wig. They went out
of the window and down the fire escape to try and get a
look in his room.

We'd have these Mercedes pulling up outside our
restaurant, with chauffeurs and televisions in them, to
take us back to our hotel. They used to think we were mad
. . . or we were pop stars. Plum and Hazel used to tell
them a different story every day. They'd tell them that I
was the Queen's mad sister and that I'd been locked up in
the mad castle all my life. 'Hello, your majesty,' they'd go.

But we always knew we were going to run out of money. One day we were tearing round doing this hotel bit, staying in massive places with posh rooms, the next we were sleeping on the beach with no money, living with all these down and outs. It was good fun, though. There were all sorts of people living on the beach, people who didn't have any money, kids that had gone to France that were on the dole, people who were escaping National Service, people from the French Foreign Legion, all sorts of people.

We met these guys called the Goolie Goolies, they were the Algerians who had a really crap time. They came over to France illegally, sneaked in, and they ended up permanently in debt to the big man who'd got them into the country. So they worked for him selling watches and plastic stuff, key-rings, having a really bad time, but they were really nice people. We were all on the same wavelength. I know it sounds ridiculous, but after the hotels, there was no pretence.

We did farm work, picking grapes. We hitched around. We stayed in some dead ropy hotels with cockroaches, and places like a disused military academy. The girls used to collect scorpions on sticks and keep them in little boxes and race them.

Once, outside Lyons, Hazel and I got abducted by some Moroccans who took us to Marseilles to sell us. That was the scariest thing that ever happened to us. Plum was staying with this man we'd met up with, we were just supposed to be going off for a couple of hours, and she was waiting for us. We could tell what was happening, they had telephones in the car and we could hear them saying they were going to sell us abroad. Hazel was probably twelve and she was a virgin so she was worth something. I don't know what I was worth, probably about three quid. But Hazel and I started screaming, going hysterical, really mad, and every time she quietened down I said, 'Keep it going, keep it going,' so they thought they'd got some spoiled English brat. We made so much racket that in the end they kicked us out. They dumped us in the dark, miles away from anywhere.

We started living in vehicles in the South of France too. One day we hitched a lift down the Côte d'Azur with someone who had a Transit. We were grape picking and he was doing the same, and the farm where we'd been picking had finished so we were on our way to the next place and we ended up going together. He had this Transit van kitted out like a camper van and we looked at it and thought, 'This is really good, isn't it?' It was hot weather so we'd just put our bags in and we started to sleep out. It was so much easier in a vehicle, getting around.

And then Frances came along. The man who had the van was the man who is Frances's dad. I got pregnant with her so we came back to England, the five of us, her dad as well. She's eight now. We were originally just coming back to England for about three weeks, but when Frances was born it turned out she had this congenital disease so we weren't able to go back, we weren't ever able to go back.

This disease is very rare. There's only, I think, seven other children who have it. It means she's on a medical diet that is very expensive. She can't eat ordinary food much, so what she eats has to be chemically and synthetically produced. It costs something like £1,000 a week to feed her.

It makes it hard to go back to France. We've been to the French health service but they said no way. We have problems finding doctors here too. It's the price of pre-scriptions, because it uses so much out of their budgets. So we get passed around. They're quite nice about it, and say, 'I'd really like to, but I'm only allowed so many thousand pounds this year and she's going to use it in a week.' There's a good doctor in Barnstable we go to, but it means that we keep having to go back to him regularly to pick up prescriptions.

So we just visit France now and we can't stay because she has to be dealt with all the time but we're hoping with this EEC-thingummy we might be able to get the medication there as well as here. It's a better place to travel, France. French people have a romantic side to them and they see it as being *mondial*, or whatever. They're much more generous as well. They'll drive on site with food and clothes and take your kids to play with their kids. Plum and Hazel were always going off on trips. 'We're going to the beach. Do your kids want to come?' You can't see that happening here. Plus the climate's a lot better as well.

After Frances was born we moved into a house in Devon, so we could stay there for a while while we got this disease regulated. It was weird, the strangest place. Three years we lived in that house and we never got to know the next door neighbours. Again the whole consumer thing that the kids were getting into seemed weird, and they were watching telly all the time. I think we just found it too hard to settle down to that kind of thing and start buying things, keeping the kids up with the clothes, Nif Naf or whatever it's called, Pumas and Reeboks and all the stuff that goes with it. We found ourselves playing that game after a few months but we were thinking, 'What are we doing? What's wrong with jumbles? They've always been all right in the past.' It had nothing to offer us. It was just depressing. Like having nothing to work for, just a giro to pay off the gas bills. And nobody ever came to see us, because they don't. It's like that, isn't it?

So I went back on the road. When you're sat in somebody's house now you think, 'God, I couldn't cope with this. I've got to get back home.' For the first few weeks it's great staying in a house – baths and washing machines and things. But after a few days you lose contact with what the weather's doing and everything. I know it sounds really dreadful, but you watch the birds and you watch the seasons and watch the weather and your perspective on life is wider. You end up with tunnel vision after being in a house for a little while. You start wondering what's on telly. Strange things.

On the road it's the opposite. Finding the time to do everything is hard. I make lists of what we're going to do.

We're always writing lists. Fix this, do that, chop wood,
but we never do them. We're really good talkers. We just
talk when we have spare time. Keeping the vehicles going
is time-consuming, but I can do it. This is a Leyland, this
one. I've had it five or six years. I've got a good set of tools
and have become quite adept at repairing most things. In
the early days I got books on basic petrol engine and
diesel engine maintenance and worked out how they
worked. The main thing is buying the bits. This one's
obsolete. But I really like it so I want to keep it going and
it's a constant search for parts.

I think I'd be old, living in a house. Not that I'm not old.
I'm forty-four which is not that old, but it is by some
people's standards. But I look at some women my age and
they're going, 'Ooh, I can't get up them steps.' Part of it's
that you eat better. You're more concerned with proper
food and when you eat it. You don't buy junk food. Apart
from the fact it's more expensive you wouldn't survive
two minutes if you didn't eat proper food.

We go where the work is. We came here for the picking:
peas, beans and raspberries. It's winter now, which isn't
the best time of year. The cauliflowers and daffodils aren't
ready yet. They don't start until January.

Travellers are just people, there are people that work
and people that don't, people that drink and people that
don't, people that fight and people that don't, and people
like us. One person does something and we're all the
same. We get branded much easier than other groups of
people. It's worse than being black a lot of the time.

I can't imagine stopping, whatever the law is. I don't
think it's just me. I think there are thousands and thousands of people who won't stop. But I'm pessimistic. I'm
sure it's going to be worse in the future than people think.
It won't just be council people coming in like that fellow,
the Gypsy Liaison Officer. They'll be coming in with riot
police and the social services. They'll take the kids, shoot
the dogs.

If they did I'd fight. I'd do whatever it takes. If you've travelled more than three or four years you are a traveller and that's what you do and it just doesn't compare with other ways of life.

JANE

At twenty-nine Jane is seven months pregnant with her second child. Her first, Dale, careers around the small caravan on a red plastic tractor. Dale's dad is six years younger than Jane. She jokes that she's obviously got some thing for younger men. Her last boyfriend was twenty-one when she left him. She's a southerner but you would never guess it from the Yorkshire accent she has acquired in the last few years.

Jane has learned about lurchers from Chen, and goes out over the fields with them every morning.

They are wintering in their caravan on the site just outside Embsay.

I'm the black sheep of the family. How could I travel when my brothers and sisters have got nice houses and jobs and 2.2 children and 2.2 dogs with a nice Fiesta? What am I doing this for when I could be in a house? But it's simple. After all, my mum did it. She was a Romany. She lived in a horse-drawn caravan and she brought up ten of us before I came along. On the tenth one they decided to go into a house so they sold the horse and the wagon, bought a two-bedroomed house, and then I came along. So I never knew the road, I only knew the stories from my mum.

I don't know where she was born. Up until I was fourteen she used to tell me her stories about what the road was like, the hardship and the good bits, but then she died. And I flipped from being a nice sweet little girl into being a rebel. I wanted out.

I come from Portland Bill in Dorset, I love that island – it's beautiful. But the rest of Dorset's rubbish. I left there when I was ten, moved to Cambridge. Did O-levels. Moved to Great Yarmouth, got married, got divorced. I spent a lot of years moving, I moved once or twice a year, but I never lived in vehicles, I'd always moved from house to flat to bedsit. I couldn't sit still. My dad lived in Yorkshire and one day I thought, 'I'm off to see him.' So I packed a rucksack, thumbed it up here and never went back.

Then about two years later I met Chen. How it came about was I lived in a house that cost me £350 a month, slogging my guts out to pay that. I was working at a chicken factory in Crosshills and I was left with nowt after I'd paid everything. After that I lived in a bedsit in an attic in Keighley which had a skylight and that was it, my only light. I didn't like it at all. So I moved into a caravan site with the help of a friend of mine who's living down in the bottom layby now, Michael, and he introduced me to Chen who was living on the site at the time. Chen was a poacher. And I decided . . . I thought, yeah, that's a man. He likes going out catching his own food. He knows what he wants out of life and I want more or less the same thing and I'd like to learn from him. So we got together and he taught me what he knows and I . . . well, I didn't know that much, so I didn't teach him anything.

Skinning rabbits, that was the first thing he taught me. The first week of going out together he took me out and we caught four rabbits. He skinned two and he said, 'Right, you do it.' And I've been doing it ever since.

Three years ago I couldn't go out and find my own food. I wouldn't know the first thing about it. I didn't have a clue how to go about catching a rabbit. But now I could survive on my own anywhere. I like my rabbit stew, I do.

Since then I've had my own apprentices, that's what I call them, friends who live on the road who want to learn and get into the lifestyle. The other day one of my apprentices cooked up a rabbit and Chen ended up with rabbit shit all in his mouth because it hadn't been cleaned properly. That apprentice is still learning.

I was basically an outsider. I was a southerner, and Chen and his friends were northerners. The first year of us being together we mouthed at each other all the time. It's got to the stage now where they've totally forgotten I'm a southerner now.

Chen and I just decided to go on the road together. It wasn't really a decision. It was a case of he got angry one day, smashed the caravan up and disappeared for two days and then came back with a puppy and said, 'Are you coming?' And I said, 'Well, I haven't got a home now, of course I'm coming!' So we ended up living in an Escort van for a while with a stove in the back and a chimney poking out of the passenger seat, two dogs on the front seat and the little puppy sleeping with us in the back. It was brilliant. It was beautiful. I didn't have the electricity bills, or any bills to worry about. All we had to think about was getting new gas bottles for the two-ring burner we cooked on. I just felt free for a change. For the first time I didn't have any ties of rent, water rates and all that. This is the life. I went on the dole, and I was getting £69 a fortnight, which was nothing compared to what I was earning at the chicken factory – up to £400 a week – but it was all mine. To me that was more money than I'd had left when I was working, and I could get up when I felt like it and go out across the fields.

When I came into this life through Chen it was what I actually had been looking for all the time, I just hadn't found anyone who wanted to share that life with me. Men I had met had always wanted houses and a nice little wifey to cook for them when they come home and I'm not that. I wanted to be out there chopping wood and struggling, because sitting in a house cooking and cleaning is mundane and it was never for me. Since the first story about life on the road got told to me by my mother when I was four or five, I've dreamt of it. So meeting Chen made that come true.

In the end that first van of ours died. It seized up. The first place we lived after that was by the reservoir on the Skipton estate, just above Chen's brother's house, just a bender against the wall for a couple of nights. Then we went over and had a site between Cross Hills and Cowling for about a week before we got evicted, and then – three years ago – we set up a bender right here in this valley, on the bottom layby, just by the wall in the field by the river.

We stayed here for a whole winter. This was where Dale was conceived. It was brilliant living in a bender. We had a double bed, we had a carpet, we had a fire and a cooker. It was quite a bad winter as well. The wind and rain comes down this valley.

We were laying in bed one morning, seven o'clock, and it seemed like the door had opened, so I said, 'Chen, get out of bed and pull that flap down.' Chen looked out and there was one of our tarpaulins about half a mile down the field. Oh shit. Never mind. Get back into bed, get down under the covers because it's pissing down. There was sleet and all sorts. Anyway, about half an hour later, woof! Off went another tarp and the only one left barely covered three-quarters of the poles we were living under. We were under the wraps thinking, 'Oh God, this is horrible.' One of our mates was living on the layby in a bus at the time. The third tarpaulin went and we were straight in there! 'We're dossing here,' we said, and just went to sleep on the floor. We waited until the weather calmed down, got a bit of dry carpet and rebuilt the bender – started again. You learn by experiment.

We moved off in the spring. The most annoying thing is the evictions. That year we got evicted twenty-eight times. I was carrying Dale. They were just going for us. If you're carrying a baby they'll give you three weeks. So if the baby is due next week they'll leave you alone, and give you two weeks after the birth until the midwife's finished. But at the same time they'll evict the rest of the site and just leave the pregnant people there.

I had Dale in Airedale Hospital. The midwives were beautiful, the best I've met. I've got the same midwife this time round for the baby I'm carrying now – the same midwife as Chris had when she had Tom last week. She lives with Zed in a bus on the lower site. It's the second baby she's had on a bus. A lot of people have their babies on buses, but I want mine in hospital so I can come home and have the fire ready. I don't want all that scrambling around you get if you have it in the caravan, all the plastic sheets and stuff. Apart from that I don't want everyone else on the site to have to put up with me screaming my head off. Some people here who've had babies on the road don't mind everyone coming round and putting their heads round the door to have a look, but I like my privacy a bit more.

This one's due first week in March.

There are things we do on regular days. Like Monday we'll get up, light the fire, Chen will take the dogs down the field while I sort out his breakfast. Then I'll go and take my dog out. There's always one of us with Dale then. After that on a Monday we'll go and change my money book, go down to Chen's mother's house and get a bath and a cup of tea, come home, light the fire, sit down and get stoned for the evening. Mondays and Fridays are set days when we'll go and have a bath at his mum's.

On other days we'll go scrapping, depending on how much there is about, we'll go and collect wood or water, go and buy and sell whatever we can. When we first came here there was a lot of wood from dead trees, but that's all gone now, so we just go down to the industrial estate and pick up a load of broken pallets.

It's not hard bringing up Dale here. It's harder in big rooms, like round Chen's mum's, because there's so many ornaments and so many things he's not allowed to touch. He gets manic and we're forever going, 'Dale, no!' Round here in our caravan he knows he's not allowed in that cupboard where some of our stuff is, and he knows he doesn't touch the cooker, but that's it more or less.

We have a lot to do with Chen's family, living round here. They love seeing Dale. I let them see him as much as they can because they're getting on and I didn't have any grandparents and I would have loved to have known them, so I like the idea of him knowing his grandparents. At first it was, 'Oh you can't have a child on the road!' But now they've seen Dale they can't wait for this one to be born. But they're super. Dale's dad in particular. He's conservative. He was very closed-minded. He was against us being on the road at all at first but now he'll stand up and say, 'Well they've *got* to find you somewhere to park.' He's round here twice, three times a week. He runs us about in his car. He's just totally changed. He's opened out. Whereas before if he'd seen anything written about his precious son in the paper it was, 'Right, I disown you. You've been in trouble with the law.' Chen spent six days in prison a couple of months back for non-payment of fines – it was motoring offences, untaxed vehicle. When I told Chen's dad his son was in prison – because he didn't know and I had to go round and tell him – he just laughed and said, 'What are *you* going to do?' I said, 'Just carry on until he comes home.' When he got out his dad brought him back here afterwards.

I'd like to stay on the road indefinitely, but it all depends on how much pressure we get from society, from the government, from the council.

Our aim is to go horse-drawn. When Dale gets a little older and the little one's a bit older too. Chen worked on an animal sanctuary that looked after cruelty cases on a community programme, so he knows a bit about horses. If you've got a horse they can't push you on because your horse has got to graze and got to water and it's a lot nicer seeing a horse grazing in your field than it is seeing a big truck stuck outside.

My mum had an easier life than we do, I think. Thirty or forty years ago with a horse-drawn you were more accepted. They used to go out scrumpin', thievin', getting potatoes from the fields, and they carried on doing that when we began living in a house. My mum had a couple of dogs. And my dad was in the army, so she spent a lot of the time in a wagon on her own. All the kids doing their own thing. She said it was hard, but they were a lot more accepted. She could go to a door and ask for bread and water and they'd give it. And you get to stay places with your horse.

She used to talk about it sometimes but I can't remember many of the stories she used to tell. I'd love to know them now.

DIXIE

To get to the site, you have to drive down the runway of the disused airfield, one of the many built in Norfolk during the Second World War. In the dark you can make out the trailers and buses parked next to a large old shed. Dixie and Dick and their six children have used this site as a base for about four years. Dick lives in the trailer with the television in it, so everyone gathers in there when there's a good film on. Dixie has her own little touring trailer, as do the oldest two children, Rollin and S.E., while the other four children sleep in a large bus. Three other travellers, Phil, Nick and Paddy, also live on site.

Dixie is in the kitchen caravan, one which used to belong to Irish travellers. It was decorated with fancy mirrors before they bought it; now it's covered in photos, postcards and children's drawings. By the stove, four young children are playing at a table. Two of them are Dick and Dixie's. Dixie's been reading them Matilda *by Roald Dahl. Now they've got out the large old rose-covered biscuit tin full of orange cardboard letters that they've cut out themselves. The kids are picking out letters from the tin and chanting the rhyme from Dahl's book, 'Mrs D, Mrs I, Mrs F-F-I, Mrs C, Mrs U, Mrs L-T- Y.'*

This trailer is just one big kitchen now and it's the most hectic and busiest in the camp. It's just a cooking area really, because there are a lot of us. We eat in here and, you know, wherever the teapot is you're bound to have a lot of people gathering.

At one time the kitchen was just at the very far end and it's had to be extended because of the amount of cooking that gets done. We have the gallery there, with all the kids' drawings and stories pinned up, that's my favourite bit of this trailer. The seat at the end here can be made into a bed, where visitors can sleep when they are staying over. We've got loads of other spaces. If what we've got now were all put together, we'd just about be living in a mansion.

I started travelling when I was eighteen, about 1970, that's when I met Dick. I was born in America and was living in Paris, and I was supposed to be going to go to art college. But then a girlfriend of mine called Beany and I went to Ireland together, and then we decided to go to Kent. I knew someone who was living there in a caravan, and a few yards up from them was Dick and his brother and loads of dogs and puppies.

I didn't take much notice of him at first. Me and Beany decided to continue our journey and go up to Scotland next, and because Dick knew someone who lived in Scotland he gave us their name and said, 'Well, while you are up there you're probably going to need this polythene, because it might rain, and some extra blankets.' So we borrowed them, and obviously we had to bring them back.

When we came back Dick was just off to the Isle of Wight festival and he asked us to go along. Beany went back to Paris but I went and fell in love with Dick. That was twenty-two years ago and we've been on the road ever since.

I'd never been to anything like it before. We went there in a little car with two little tents. It was a big hippie festival, Jimi Hendrix and all that, great fun, especially as I hadn't long been away from home and school.

I had an American passport so it was more convenient for us to get married. For a while we lived in a commune in the middle of nowhere near Carmarthen, then, before I turned twenty-one, we went to Ireland and stayed there nearly thirteen years travelling around. While we were there, Dick started buying horses, and he bought this lovely old four-wheeled cart, like the original Bill Wrighttype potter's cart, that's the type with the bow top. He bought it at Ballinasloe Fair and he was in love with it. He rebuilt the top and we wintered in that.

The following spring I was pregnant with S.E. and my parents turned up. I hadn't seen them for ages and my mum was saying, 'You can't live in a wagon if you're going to have a baby, we'll get you a piece of land.' I didn't think that Dick would ever like that idea at all, but he knew of five acres of land that was for sale in Kenmare, County Kerry. A friend of his owned the land that was adjoining it. So they bought this land for us with a derelict house on it, and we arrived there about a week before S.E. was born.

At one point, for a short while, we did live upstairs in the house, but Dick never did anything to it. He made all these wonderful barns for the horses, and he made beautiful twisted hedges out of willow and roses and blackcurrants, and he did great things with the land, but he just could not wrap his head around that house.

We stayed there two summers. It was all right, and some of the neighbours were very very nice, but some did not take to us at all. There was one man down the valley who despised us. He didn't like the idea of tinkers pulling into the old valley where his family had lived for generations. He made our life very difficult and poisoned our dogs and all kinds of other things. Another guy a few houses down was also very unpleasant. He jumped out on me one day when I was cycling back from town and tried to stop me, and he had his trousers round his ankles. He was a real creep. I thought, 'How are we going to live here and bring up S.E.?'

So we left there, but that was the closest we ever got to living in a house. We continued on our travels and for seven years we only went about in horse-drawn wagons.

Next came Rollin and he was born in Bantry in West Cork. All that summer I'd been really pregnant and it had been wonderful, lying in the sun, swimming and drawing. Dick and his brother Gary had been out fishing every day and S.E. just loved the beach. That summer is one of my fondest memories of travelling. Just before he was born we were in a wagon and I decided that I wanted to find someone with a house where I could have him. I kind of asked around for somewhere and I met this nice woman who said that I could have the baby in her house. She lived on her own with two teenage daughters, and she ended up delivering Rollin herself because the midwife was sick and the doctor was tied up. I stayed there for a couple of months and Dick was in a wagon down the road with S.E. So that was Rollin. Roxy was born in 1979, when we were parked in the midlands near a village called Bracknagh in County Offaly, by which time we'd got a big trailer.

Travelling with three young children was not much of a problem. They were healthy, and I was happy and really into what I was doing, learning how to do everything, cooking and baking on the fire. I turned it into an art. It was something I really wanted to be able to do.

Dick used to earn bits of money but we never had much. I think we went on the dole after the first year. I used to hate that. I've never been proud of it, but all the people we travelled with, I'm afraid most of them drew dole. They were all these talented people, they could all do things, but there wasn't a hell of a lot of ambition around.

I've done lots of little things to earn money all along. Never could you say that I came anywhere near to earning a living but I was always up to something or other, making ointments and having stalls at fairs with herbal lotions and potions.

At one time we got together this travelling show in Ireland called 'Shamrock Commotions' with a big marquee and a band. It had a café as well and we did some children's theatre. I danced solidly for the next three or four months, not professionally or anything, just to the band. I was pregnant again, and I can remember dancing with Rollin in my arms. I've had dancing all around me all my life.

The big caravan we got after Roxy was born got destroyed. It was being towed by a lorry driven by a friend of ours, came off the tow-hitch and went off the side of the road. So Dick went off and bought a bus. In those days people didn't live in buses like they do now, but he had this idea that it might just work. We converted it all and put in this lovely little stove called 'The Enchantress', a small range in that sort of flowery cast-iron work. We had bought it years before this but it really come into its own on that bus.

In the big bus, we pulled up at this beautiful place between Kenmare and Killarney called 'Ladies View', and decided to have the baby there. I found a midwife in Killarney who had had experience in California in all sorts of wild places and she was all for it. But Pearly was born, · very, very quickly, just before the midwife got to us, so my friend Ruth delivered her. She still had her cord and all that business when the midwife arrived but she was there. Dick wasn't around, he was off in Casteltownbere, so he missed the whole event and when he got home there was Pearly. She was three weeks early, due in the new year and it was only December 20th, so he was quite surprised.

That night some friends of ours turned up. They had been poaching and they had caught this salmon far bigger than my newborn Pearly. I can just remember lying on the bed with this little baby and seeing this huge silver salmon shining above me and the guy holding it saying, 'Look what we've got for Pearly's birthday supper.'

We stayed there about a year and then we went to Tipperary and I had a baby that died. He would have been about nine by now.

Wanda was born in Thurles hospital in Tipperary. Well, when I say 'in the hospital', she was actually born in the back of a van on the way to the hospital. I had this series of children that just shot out like rockets, never where or when they were supposed to. At 2 a.m. we were rushing along to this hospital with Wanda being born, and Dick went charging in and banged on the door and he was

yelling, 'Hurry up, my wife is having a baby *now*!' The
poor old midwife came rushing out and I was in the back
of a van with the door open and she literally just delivered
Wanda there with her stainless steel bowl under her arm.
If she had been five seconds later it would have been my
friend Ruth delivering the baby again.

I went into the hospital for the night and the next
morning I had one of the few arguments I've ever had
with anyone. We were the only mother and baby in the
hospital and Wanda had been born at about 2.45 a.m. The
next morning she was lying there blissfully asleep and
this nurse came trotting along and picked her up and
woke her up and said, 'It's bath time.' I said, 'But she's
asleep.'

'Never mind. Time to bath the babies is ten o'clock.' Off
she went down the corridor with my Wanda. Wanda was
my fifth child, so I was a bit achy and I couldn't just jump
up and give chase but I eventually got down the corridor
and found my poor little baby screaming herself blue in
the face, getting scrubbed with soap.

I was furious. I told her that there was no need for this,
that I didn't do that to my babies and I didn't want her
washed. The nurse said, 'While she's in the hospital she's
my child and this is what we do.' I grabbed Wanda out of
her arms and as soon as Ruth arrived I went home. I had
to sign the papers saying I was being irresponsible.

That was November 1984. The following spring we
came back to England and travelled with two musician
friends of ours. My last child, Zeeta, was born in Shrews-
bury, in 1986, and shortly after that we came to Norfolk
because I got a job. We had this beautiful four-wheeler
that Dick had largely built and restored and then I painted
it and it was really rather nice. Some friends of ours got us
a job at a fair in Geldeston clearing the rubbish with our
four-wheeler, because it was a small fair and they wanted
it to be all ethnic and nice, and they didn't want any big
lorries driving on to the site.

It was really easy work, a few times a day you had to go
round with the horse and collect the bags and put them in

a skip. We did the same at a fair at Tuttington, and did some music and singing and ran a café. We still have a marquee that we take around during the summer to fairs. We generally stay quite local, there are so many things going on around here in the summer.

Most of the schooling of the children, I've done myself. The children get involved in a lot of things, and there have always been plenty of people around to teach them. Ray, one of the men with us now, he teaches them maths, and at one time there was an ex-schoolteacher who came and taught them reading. We had a lady in Norwich who used to come out who was really interested in teaching them and Tim Everson, who works for the Travellers' Education Service in Suffolk, comes up. Most of it, though, I've done myself. It's something I had intuitively. It's not difficult, it's just having the time. I don't have half enough time.

Some of them take to it and some of them don't. S.E. and Roxy know a lot, but Rollin is really not that bothered. He's learned how to read, and he reads well, but his writing is atrocious for a fifteen-year-old. He just prints and he doesn't spell very well, but I can't force him to get interested in it. It doesn't worry me. I've put it to him lots of times that he should go to school and learn how to do it properly, but he doesn't want to and I wouldn't ever make him. He can do so many things and I don't think he'll ever be held back by it. I mean, he plays the guitar really well, he can handle horses and dogs and he can do mechanics and electrics. He's got oceans of practical knowledge and common sense. Roxy's younger than him and she reads and writes perfectly because she's really interested in it. Pearly's reading 90 per cent fluently, but it's a bit more difficult to focus her on her work. I'm working on improving her writing. At the moment she still mixes up capital letters and small letters.

When S.E. was thirteen she said she wanted to go to school, and that was all right by me, because I don't like sending them when they're little, but I thought she was old enough to say she wanted to go. S.E. proved that you can get in there and catch up.

I went when I was four until I was eighteen, five days a week. It's just so total, isn't it? Most of the day isn't spent learning anything except how to be at school, how to be obedient, which is useful up to a point, but you miss out on all the things you can do at home. I sat at my desk and looked out of the window and felt like I was in prison. If there was a school where they'd teach my children to read and write and then let them off, or encourage them in what they like without forcing all the other stuff down their necks I'd be delighted.

I don't like the way school categorises children. Roxy would probably be considered bright because she likes the school work, and Pearly would be considered slow because she's dreamy and imaginative. I think that's terrible. School makes your children into products, grades them and gets them competing against each other.

About four or five years ago we got our first ever, ever television. I was watching it one night, it was an 'Arena' programme about flamenco dancing and I thought, 'That looks the business.' I said to Dick I wanted to learn how to do that, and he laughed. I mentioned it to a friend of mine the next day and she immediately said the name of a woman in Norwich who taught flamenco. So I found her and went to Norwich with Roxy and S.E. to start learning it. S.E. only did it for a few weeks, then decided it wasn't her thing, but Roxy took to it. Then Rollin decided to learn flamenco guitar, then Pearly decided to learn flamenco guitar too and all the little ones have started to learn how to dance as well.

One day, I would really like, if they are willing, to have our own group to dance and play music together. I'd really love that.

S.E.

S.E. (pronounced Essey) is Dixie and Dick's eldest daughter. She was born in Kenmare in Eire in 1975. She lives in her own trailer parked up near her parents' caravan. While her mother prepares a rabbit stew, S.E. is working at her sewing machine. She is doing a course in textiles.

Some of my earliest memories of travelling are the horses, working the horses with my dad. The first time I ever rode a horse on my own was when I was three, and I can remember Dad letting us go by the bus so Mum could see me. That was the first time I rode all by myself, without him holding on. It was in Tipperary, I would guess. I remember when I was really young, Mum doing my hair, reading to me and teaching me rhymes.

When I was thirteen I decided that I wanted to go to school because I didn't know anyone my own age. There wasn't anything happening that really grabbed me. I thought that maybe there was something in school, and I should do it, just in case there was.

The school was in Diss. I enjoyed learning, even though it was hard work, but school wasn't fun because I just didn't get on with any of the kids. I mean, there was one girl I used to see a bit. We were complete opposites. She wanted to be a policewoman but she couldn't because she wasn't tall enough and her eyesight wasn't good enough. She didn't have any friends, so we used to hang around together. She moved to the other side of the country quite early on, after about three months or so.

Looking back on it, I remember school as the worst couple of years of my life. Definitely.

They seemed to think that because I was a traveller I was different. I mean, if I had gone in there and said, 'Oh, I'm a traveller, but I'd much rather be like you,' it might have been different. But I'm not like them and I don't really want to be. I was perfectly happy the way I was, that was the bit everyone found a bit strange. They knew I was doing things that were completely different. They were interested, but they weren't, like, grown-up enough to come and say, 'Could you tell me about yourself?' I guess they just took the piss really. It was not very nice at all.

I was really into motorbikes at the time. I didn't seem to be into anything that quite fitted. They just couldn't accept me for what I was.

The last year, we had this new headmaster, and he was all right, he was into the arts and all that. I wrote to him and told him everything that had been going on, and how much I wanted to be in school and the plans that I had, but that I thought it would be better if I only came in for some classes. He was really helpful. Mind you, I also said to him that if he tried to make me come to all the classes I'd go back to Ireland. He decided that getting an education was the main thing, so he let me. You couldn't explain that to the kids, though. You couldn't tell them that the situation wasn't working out for me. That last year I only did five classes, five different subjects, and then went home. I didn't see any of the kids at all and that was better. They hated it. Suddenly there was a real reason for not liking me, because I had all these different rules to all of them which they thought was really, really not fair and not on. Fair enough I suppose, but if it hadn't been for them I probably wouldn't have done it.

Teachers were coming up and saying, 'Look, all right, you hate being in school. Try this, it will make it easier for you.' The kids of course thought I got all this extra help because I was a traveller, and that just was not true. Yes, I had help but I passed my GCSEs fairly and anyone who says differently is mad. I did all the work, I sat at home for hours and hours and hours working and it wasn't easy.

After that I went to college in Norwich which is a lot bigger. The thing is, once you get to that age and go to college, you start to meet people who aren't like everything you've always known. Anything at all different is considered quite exciting, so there I was, I was different and I was exciting. I made loads of friends at college and I've still got lots of really good friends from there. But at school . . . there's something about school, everyone is so similar. People are all really different once you get to know them, but at school everyone seems the same. There was me doing all sorts of strange stuff that made no sense to them at all.

Diss is a very small town, very old-fashioned, quiet and not really my sort of place. I hardly know anyone there now; maybe because I went to school there I avoid it. I went into Diss when I was at college and saw a load of boys from my school. They said, 'What are you doing now?' When I said I was at college they said, 'Naaah, sod off!' They just didn't believe me. It's their problem, anyway. It's a bit hard to convince yourself of that at the time because there are hundreds of them and only one of you, but it is their problem. Definitely.

I had a birthday party not very long ago and I invited lots of my friends – college friends, really old friends my mum and dad's age, people my age who are travellers and people I've met in Diss or Norwich. I didn't invite any kids from school. It was weird. They all stayed in their groups. There was no mixing at all. I found it very strange, and they found it difficult too. If you are at a party and everyone's a traveller, or everyone lives in a house, there's no problem about mixing. I was rushing around trying to introduce them to each other, it was terrible. I don't really mix too much these days. I think about it a lot more if I'm going out with people or having people here. I make sure they all know each other first.

I left college last June. I should have gone back this year, but I decided I wasn't going to. My plan now is to get a

Prince's Trust grant to set up a screen-printing workshop
so I can print T-shirts. I'm doing a textiles course which is
all home study apart from once a month when you go and
meet lots of people on the same course. It's really good
because you know that you have something to work
towards, and you can do it when you want and where you
want. On the course you learn how to put patterns
together, about printing, dying, all the basic stuff. I
already know quite a lot about screen-printing and I've
done quite a bit of air-brushing. Eventually I want to make
and print my own clothes, not just T-shirts. I want to
design the sort of clothes I like to wear, because I never
wear T-shirts, you see. It could be really good. I am
working quite hard at it.

Of course, one day I'm going to have a cottage in the
mountains with a waterfall, and roses, and a garden.
That's going to be somewhere foreign, where it's warm
in the winter. I like travelling, because I don't like being
in one place very much. I'm going to have somewhere
to come and visit in Norfolk, and I'm going to have
something big and movable, a really nice big Carlite
or something like that. I do like the idea of having a
base, hot water and baths, and a washing machine, and
an iron, and one of those things for making swirly hot
chocolate drinks.

I definitely want to have kids, but I wouldn't put them
in to school at first. I'd teach them how to read and write
first and once they got to be about twelve I'd make them
take some sort of education. Ideally I'd have teachers
come in and teach them or take them to classes, because I
don't think you can learn everything at home. I'd travel
around with them a lot and show them all sorts of things,
and anything they showed an interest in I would encourage. If there's a lot happening around you, you don't need
too much school as a child. School doesn't teach you to be
an individual. In fact it teaches you to be the complete
opposite. Only when you're older and know what you're
about, then I think you would stand a chance of getting
something good from it.

As a young child, school will do nothing at all for you apart from make you pick up bad habits and behave strangely and want to be the same as everyone else. That's what I've learnt.

PART SIX

THE END OF THE ROAD

DYLAN

*There's a Rizla paper stuck on the appropriate doorbell saying:
Dylan De Viant. The Dylan he was born with, the rest he picked
up. 'I was called Deviant for a while. When it's written down,
nobody spots it. That's just a bit of fun, it amuses me.'*

*He's dossing in a flat in Brighton. The bulb's gone in the front
room, so has the washer on the tap in the adjoining kitchenette;
water pours out.*

*Dylan was adopted. One of his earliest memories is standing at
a bus stop with his mother and being frightened as he watched the
carpet factories at Kidderminster turn out for lunch when the
twelve o'clock hooter went: 'It looked like people pouring out of a
machine.' He believes the scene had a lasting effect on him. 'I
couldn't see myself working at a steady job.'*

*He went to prep school at Malvern, but got expelled. After that
he went to a Rudolf Steiner school and then the local secondary
modern. From the age of sixteen he worked with a PA company
called LSD, touring with Mud, Sweet, Gary Glitter, Queen, 'and
some good bands as well, like Nazareth and David Bowie in '72'.
In the seventies he wrote a book called* Diary of a Rock 'n' Roll
Roadie *at the suggestion of Mott the Hoople's Ian Hunter, who
had written a successful book called* Diary of a Rock 'n'Roll
Star. *Dylan sent his manuscript off to a publisher, but heard no
more of it.*

*He went on the road after visiting Stonehenge in 1976. At the
time he was married with a newly born baby, living in a small
council flat in the Midlands. Without telling his wife, Raine, he
bought a twenty-four foot Leyland bus for about £500. When he*

*showed it to her and told her his plans for going on the road
together, she was horrified. Instead, they split up and he went on
the road on his own. In the end he raffled the bus at Inglestone
Common in 1977 for almost £2,000.*

*Dylan is a veteran of the Beanfield ('I've blanked a lot of it out.
It scared the shit out of me,') and Stoney Cross.*

*He has been to prison a few times, has had a string of
prosecutions for driving while banned and he's been through
periods of alcoholism. He's come off the road for a bit to try and
get his life organised, but he's not finding it easy and misses the
life. He's got a stash of old photos of buses he's owned, benders
he's lived in, friends he's made.*

Actually, one of the things I miss most is just taking a
dump, squatting down outdoors. In the winter of
86/87 I lived in this big bender in the woods in Wales.
There were two streams, one for washing, one for drinking out of. One night I went for a dump just the other side
of the streams in the place where I used to go wooding. I
was squatting there and I looked up and I saw this
beautiful fox coming towards me, following a trail. I
couldn't have moved if I wanted to, I wasn't in any
position to stand up if you know what I mean. The fox had
its big winter coat on and it came right up to me. All it did
was follow the trail. It came right up to me, walked round,
and then picked up the trail again. And just as it was
walking off it looked round at me. I swear it wagged its tail
at me, then wandered off into the woods. It was magical.

Myself, I like woodland sites. I like smaller sites. That
time in Wales was one of the best winters I'd ever had. I
had been at Stoney Cross in the summer. That winter I
went to Wales to stay in a friend's caravan in the woods
near Cenarth in Dyfed. She had got it together with a guy
and they were living in a bender. There were a few people
there in benders. I didn't know them well at first. There
was a reasonable-size bender there which became almost
like a hall. Everybody ate in there and we had a big fire
too.

We had permission to be on the land from the land-owner, but the neighbours were complaining and eventually we got moved off. That's when we first got the idea for the mega-bender. We were all going to spend the winter together, so we thought we might as well build one big bender. We bought this Leyland D Series flat-bed lorry and we put all the tarps and poles off there and we found this other spot.

The original idea was we were going to call it Jeremy the Doughnut-block Bender. In the comic *2000 AD* there's the Judge Dredd strip and all the apartment blocks have names like that. We were all big Judge Dredd fans. The idea was that we'd make a big circle for the interior, and then make banana-shaped pods round the outside of it so it was just two circles, one inside the other like a dough-nut.

The site we found was near Eglwyswrw, seven or eight miles away from Cardigan. We had some vigilantes there at first. We'd just started to get the poles up and this English landowner came up and said, 'You can't do that here.'

And we said, 'Yes we can, we've got permission off that guy who owns that holiday cottage. He lives in Birmingham.'

Not true of course, though we had heard that he lived in Brum. The man came back twenty minutes later and said, 'No you ain't got permission. I've been on the phone and checked. You're getting out of here.'

We had this guy with us called Welshman. He said, 'Who're you telling to leave? I'm Welsh and you're English. Piss off out of my country.' Giving it all of that. We said, 'If you want us to leave, take us to court, evict us properly.'

And he said, 'We'll see about that. We'll soon get you out of here.' And then he pissed off, which left us wondering what he was going to do. We went to the police and they said, 'Nothing we can do until he's done something.'

So we came back to the site and it started to get dark between three and four in the afternoon, so we decided we were going to build a big fire and sit outside. We trotted around the woods to find these big sticks, some of them we put lump hammer heads on.

There was only one way on to this site, down a track and through the gate. By the time these fourteen rugby-player-style people came on, some with handkerchiefs around their faces, they were confronted by nine of us, six blokes and three women. We got the girls to get into the lorries and the vans and turn the lights on. They'd been in the pub and we'd been able to hear them coming down the track, so they were confronted by six blokes, stripped to the waist, with big weapons. One of us was doing fire-eating, breathing fire at them.

They went, 'What? We've only come for a chat, lads.' There was a bit of shouting from both sides and then they all pissed off. No problem.

Anyway, the next morning this Land-Rover pulled up and this farmer type stepped out, a big man in his sixties. His arms were like my legs. Welsh. And he said, 'Where's the rest of you then? I had the local rugby team last night in my house saying they were going to come and sort out some hippies, and they were back in half an hour with their tails between their legs and I wanted to see what frightened them off.' He was all right, he came inside the bender we were building and he was right impressed with it. Webb, I think his name was. He said, 'If you have any trouble phone me and I'll sort them out.'

So far so good. That afternoon, though, it started pissing down. And somewhere downstream from where we were one of the sluice gates was shut. Now if we'd looked properly at the grass we would have noticed it was very long and weedy where this stream went round the patch of land we were on in a bit of a swansneck. The area we were on began to backfill with water. Somebody was in the kitchen end of the bender and said, 'Oi! We've got water in here.' So we dived out and half the field was flooded and within about a minute it had come right up to where we had the fire. So we grabbed the bedding and left anything that didn't matter. We had a Subaru four-wheel drive and got that on to dry land, and the lorry and the van, and then spent a night in the bloody shed of the holiday cottage wondering what we were going to do the next day.

Fortunately, we had a friend who lived in Nevern about three miles away and she put us up for a couple of days until we got everything dried out, and we heard about a bit of land that somebody's mother had where it would be all right to build the big bender. This time we had time to plan it out. It was across two fields to get there, so it was quite a distance from the road.

We made a splendid job of it. We got there about December 3rd, and started building it about the 5th or 6th and it took us about three days. It was quite a feat of engineering, because we didn't use any rope or string, except for the ones we used to tie down the tarps on the outside. It was solid as a rock. I used to have a photograph of seven of us sitting on top of it passing the drink around.

We measured it in Dyls – Dylans – because I know I'm five foot ten, and it turned out to be twenty-seven-and-a-half foot long by about twenty-three or -four foot wide and twelve and a half foot on the top. When they eventually moved off there, they put all the tarps and poles on to the lorry and took it over to a weighbridge and I think it worked out at three-quarters of a ton.

We had a big open fire in the middle which was our heating and cooking fire, with a big tea kettle on top of it constantly, and five pods off the main circle for couples to sleep in. One of the pods we turned into a brewery, brewing our own brew from kits and adding extra hops and sugar to make it quite a potent brew. By then we'd grown to fifteen people from the nine we started off in. It became a rule that single men slept in the living area and couples had a bit of privacy. I suppose it's a bit like living in a bedsit with paper-thin walls. You can hear the couple next door and you know what's going on, but you don't sit and listen to it, do you? I was having a long-term relationship with a girl in Brighton at the time, and she came to visit a couple of times but she was shy. So the sexual side of our relationship didn't work well there. We had to take ourselves off into the woods. A bit cold, but we managed.

We were there quite a long while. It was like a nice little family. We all ate together, vegetarian food, so that the vegetarians and everyone could eat. If you wanted to dive into town for a bacon sarnie, fair enough. At the time we were all signing on the dole – we got seven giros one week and the rest the next, so it worked out really nicely. It was a giro in the health shop for pulses and things, a giro in the off-licence, a couple of giros in the supermarket. We had an arrangement with the local wholesaler in Cardigan, buying two sacks of spuds, a net of onions, a net of carrots, sprouts, leeks, and once we'd been doing this for a while he started saving all the bruised fruit he wasn't going to sell, putting it all in a big box and giving it to us for a couple of quid. If you needed a pair of boots or a pair of long johns, that was fair enough, buy them with your giro, but the rest went into the pot. We lived together, ate together, and looked after each other.

We were miles from anywhere and you had to get this woodpile together. We'd end up competing with each other, walking four or five miles with huge great logs and somebody else would chop it up.

I think that was one of the most pleasant times. Nobody was ever hungry, there was always tobacco for a smoke, there was always a cup of tea going and something to do.

I do find it quite difficult to adapt to living in a town environment, because living on a site you've got your mates around you. I find it strange knowing quite a few people around Brighton and thinking, 'Oh, I haven't seen so-and-so around for ages, now where do they live? Oh Christ, it's at the other end of town.' I admit that most of my social life here is spent in pubs, which is one of the things I didn't want to get back into, because I suppose I am an alcoholic. But living in a town, that's what you tend to do. I don't think I'd drink so much on a site. There's other things to do.

The first few nights I spent in Brighton, in a place up the road, I couldn't sleep. Even now I don't feel comfortable. This is an alright place to live but at the end of the day it's not mine. Even if I was leaseholder or tenant it wouldn't be mine. There's a claustrophobia. In my room I have to have the window open day and night, even if it's cold outside. I've got to have fresh air, as fresh as I can get in Brighton, anyway.

There's more people now who are just rebelling. People don't seem to have the respect. You walk around a town these days and it's full of litter. There are bins but they don't use them. I've seen squats in Brighton where they burn the banisters and the floorboards when it gets cold. That's not respect, is it?

Oh, I haven't left it. I'm just trying to do something else for a bit. I write poems and songs and I'm trying to get that in order. I write what I see. I pen a few lines and work on it later.

I can't say travelling has made me a better person, because I know in a lot of ways it hasn't. I have alienated myself from this society and I find it very difficult to fit in now. But I've done it myself.

I don't see this period I'm in at the moment as being the end of my travelling days, because it's in me. I've been pacing round Brighton thinking, 'Get a caravan, get back on site.'

But I think right now I've got to have a structure in my life. I don't know . . . it's just something I have to do at the moment.

DON

It's a grey Sunday and Don is bored. There's nothing to do when it's raining like this. He wanders over to one of the caravans where someone's bought some Special Brews, buys one for a pound, and listens to the younger travellers mouthing off to each other. But that's boring too. So he wanders back to the trailer he shares with his girlfriend Paula, a dog that's half-alsation, half-lurcher, and a cat. Paula's not in.

These days he gets bored when he doesn't have any work. He applied for a job building Sizewell B. A few years ago he would have been against it, but now he says if he doesn't do it, someone else will. Paula and he don't see eye to eye on that, but he didn't get the job anyway.

It's a 1960s caravan, parked on the site by the perimeter fence of the RAF Woodbridge airbase in Suffolk. On the bench seat is a copy of the local newspaper. It's open at the classified page. Houses to let. Six or seven adverts have been ringed in biro.

Maybe I'm growing out of it. I couldn't really tell you. I'm twenty-seven now, I was sixteen when I got into the whole kind of head scene. I suppose I could be growing out of it, but I'd like to think I'm not.

If you ask me, I'm giving up because I can see that in the next two years it's going to be even harder than it is now to live like this. With the proposed changes to the law, the reform of the '68 Caravan Sites Act, as far as I can see it's Germany 1932, only not as extreme. They're not going round gassing us, or beating us up – although they *have* beaten us up before, obviously – but travelling is going to be too hard to do. I'm making my life difficult for myself by choosing to live like this.

Another reason I'm getting out is I haven't the attitude to the system I used to have. You can fight them from the outside, which is what I suppose I've been doing, or you can disappear and seem to be playing the game. A lot of the younger travellers, guys with an attitude, will say, 'Oh, you're just going along with the system.' But that's all right. It takes all sorts. Sometimes I get pissed and listen to some Levellers music and I think, oh yeah, I want to get back, buy a bus and show a lot of people we don't have to be put down for this and that. But then I've got my life to get on with.

I think it's probably not going to be easy for us to get a house. I can get a job round here OK. The sort of job I'm capable of doesn't require that kind of respect from people. I've got a good name in the local area with local employers, with the local welders, the local scrap merchants . . . the local pubs. I'm not banned from any pubs, though we've got a lot of people on site who are. If I go into town I change my clothes and have a wash, whereas other people on the site, like him over there in that caravan, he's like I was five, six years ago. Like a bull in a china shop. Which is fair enough, I can see that. The initial fun of it was a couple of years of partying, taking loads of drugs, hanging around.

I've got a bit of money from this bike accident I had years ago. I'm never skint and there's always the dole. I finished work three weeks ago making trussed roof rafters. Since I've been a traveller I've just been a labourer. All I know is how to get dirty. I told myself when I signed off last time I'd never do it again, but why not, if someone's offering you £40 a week to do nothing.

But I'm a much better person in myself if I work. Like I got up this morning quite late, half nine, ten o'clock, ambled out, nothing much to do, had breakfast, went out, had a look at a couple of boats with a friend who's thinking of buying one, dossed about. There's not much to do.

I play a bit of guitar. I used to play a lot more. Lack of inspiration. I've got a Fender Strat in the cupboard, and a Peavey amp. I used to go busking with an acoustic but I haven't busked for years now. I play anything I can sing to. I play blues. I can do a little bit of jazz guitar. I don't do enough. I like a lot of punk music. It's the anarchistic thing I like.

Ideally it's great doing nothing. Some people can do it all the time. Some people have no ambition. Like Rabbit, he's a lovely bloke, but he has no ambition. Rabbit does no one no harm, never puts anyone's nose out of place, he sticks around to help you out, he's a great bloke. No ambition.

I'm out for me really. I'm not a selfish person, don't get me wrong, you ask anyone on this site, I'll do anything for anyone, but in the end me and Paula do what's best for us. Living on the road making a statement all the time is boring. Maybe I've got older, maybe I've grown out of it, I don't know. I've come to a point in travelling where I'm just bored. I've seen as much as I want to see of 'new age travellers'. I hate that cliché 'new age'.

I lived in a place called Huntingdon when I was a kid, moved out to a village. Fields all around. Did a couple of years at agricultural college, a City and Guilds in engineering, welding, basic maintenance, ploughing.

RAF Molesworth was nearby. It was an American base in the Second World War. For years we used to go up there. It was just an old airfield and a few bunkers. We used to go up there with the motorcycle club, when I was thirteen, fourteen.

I got into motorbikes because of a love of motorcycles, not for the hard man image. We tried that on a bit when we were sixteen, seventeen, but we were never serious about it. Smoked a lot of pot, got laid back, did nothing, we were really nice people. In many ways I was a lot nicer person than I am now. I found living on the road you get this really hard edge because you need that to survive. But we were getting plenty of shit even then because I reckon quite honestly the bikers have had a harder time of it than anyone else.

First time I went to Stonehenge was in 1984, got into a bit of dope and a bit of speed, nothing heavy. I lived in a caravan with some friends for a couple of months. That was a real adventure. That was the first time away from my parents when I was seventeen. When I came back I went up to Molesworth, to the peace camp they had set up there in 1984. We used to go and score a bit of pot from the place because it was cheap. I shouldn't be telling you this, really.

The travellers moved on there because there was rumours they were going to turn it into an American silo base. Whether it was or not, I don't know. After they moved the peace camp off there were cement lorries going in there for two years, and there was a lot of local work up there, but they never put any missiles there in the end, so they tell us, and there's nothing there now.

It wasn't until the eviction of Molesworth that I realised what was going on, what I was up against, what the system was.

I was there the night before because I had some friends who had just bought this old Commer walk-through and gone up there. They were a nice bunch of people, into sitting around and getting stoned, making their way as best they could. I'd left at half past eleven because I used to live three miles down the road. At half past twelve, the camp was surrounded by these policemen. I think there was about eight hundred people involved, five hundred Commandos or some army group, Royal Engineers I think it was, who had arrived to put a fence up round Molesworth, three hundred policemen, and all these bulldozers and diggers. They just turned up in the middle of the night. There was no eviction notices. They threatened people with bulldozers, big Macks and stuff, the sort they use for motorways, and bulldozed their buses into the ground and pushed them out on to the road. The Royal Engineers started putting up the fences right away.

I used to work down the road. First thing I found out about it was half past seven in the morning when I turned up and there was a police roadblock across the road. I realised what was happening. Instead of going by I pulled in to see everyone on the site. There was still a couple of buses they were towing around trying to get them started so I turned up and asked if there was anything I could do. Of course being a biker the police gave me loads of grief. It was then I made my mind up and decided I was going to do something about what was happening in this country.

It was a decision. It was right and wrong. It was good and evil. It was that strong. Anyone who was slightly spiritual, or slightly feeling, they could see that there was a line to be drawn there. They were standing there in their black suits with their riot shields, with their batons, with their commanders, with their orders, not even knowing why they were there and what they were doing. And you'd see a few long-haired people with bright coloured jackets ambling around playing music, sitting round fires, smoking a bit of dope, having a laugh, being good people, helping each other out. And then twenty, thirty foot away you've got a line of five hundred riot shields and three hundred more round the corner on standby. I would like to think I was an anarchist back then. It was an anarchy thing.

As I said, I had this big bike smash. It was an American serviceman in a left-hand-drive Volvo, coming down the road and there was this line of traffic. I was going slow at the time but he pulled out to overtake, knocked me right . on to the other side of the road. I spent two months in hospital and lost part of my leg, you can see the scar now. I broke all my toes and there were burns on my shoulder. I was lucky, actually. I couldn't walk properly for a long time but I was already having a go on me mate's bike before I could. That was a time for ego. The driver's insurance company offered me seven grand and the solicitor said take it, so I had a bit of money.

A couple of friends and I bought a bus. We got it from this bloke called Albion Dave. It was a real hippie wagon, as ratty as any bus you'd find on the road, a 1960 Super-vega. We didn't do a lot to it, just slung a couple of double beds in the back, one at the front, and put a couple of logburners in it. We had a big range, one of the Agas. And then we all went and signed on.

It was then when we heard about the Beanfield. I think the whole thing with the police started in 1984 with Nostell Priory, then there was the Beanfield in '85. We saw that happening and that was it, we drove down to Savernake. Initially it brought everyone together. The more pressure the police put on, the more violence they showed, the better and the more communal spirit there was on site. That's when we entered on to the scene. We were welcomed with open arms. Everyone was falling over themselves to help each other, to show us the crack, what was going on, how to do this or that. These days I don't know if you'd be welcomed that way. So we latched on to this Peace Convoy. It was good. It was getting away, the first time I'd been away from home permanently and it was great.

I sold that first bus in the end. After that it was two years with nothing but a bag and a guitar, running round festival sites, squatting people's vehicles. That was the best time of my life, when I had nothing at all and lived on the road with my bag and suitcase. I had dreadlocks down to my arse. All I was interested in was smoking dope and drinking beer and getting out of my head. I knew every-body. There was some sites we'd get five hundred people on them, maybe two hundred vehicles, and I could walk on every vehicle and I'd know someone and if I didn't know them I soon would.

We went to all the festivals, we did the whole circuit for years. In '86 we all ended up at Stoney Cross. After they impounded all the vehicles there we all decided to march to Glastonbury. The press loved that. I never made it there, I got arrested for obstruction by this policeman who was escorting us for trying to leave the march and buy a cup of tea. They drove me off to Portsmouth and kept me in the cells for thirty-six hours. Afterwards I went back to

Glastonbury and met up with everyone who had walked from Stoney Cross. It's a long way, I tell you. I'm bloody glad I got arrested.

I could live on nothing in those days. You can do skips and supermarkets. There's always people on site who've got a dinner going or who will give you a cup of tea. I used to get my giro and spend it the same day down the pub, then I wouldn't think about money for the rest of the week. It's surprising how little food you can get by on. I lived on hardly anything for years. I wouldn't say I was fit and healthy. There was a time when I had body lice, head lice, nowhere to live, nothing to eat, but still I could walk in anywhere, get fed, get looked after. I'm a born moaner, but quite honestly, if I look back over the years I don't think I've ever had a grim time.

I got back into buses for a bit. The second bus I had was a 1957 AEC Reliance chassis with a Weymann body, which was a proper bus body. That was a beautiful bus. I only had it four or five months. And then I met Paula, my girlfriend, on a site. She'd been on the road a couple of years. She had been going out with someone else but they split up. Fate I suppose you could call it.

Paula and me bought a bus together, another 1962 Vega, a right heap really but we kept it going. We probably did 50,000 miles in it going up to Scotland and all around most counties in the country. We did that until 1988 and then sold it at a festival to a girl for £1,800, which is a lot more money than I'd paid for it.

Travelling around all the time was brilliant, I've been out of the scene now for a while. I don't consider myself a traveller any more because I just move around this area of Suffolk.

I've got a really good standard of living now, compared to how I used to live, on the road. We eat well. Dog eats well. Cat eats better than we do. We get on. Got a generator, chainsaw, tools. This was my ideal position. Now I've got it, I'm leaving.

In all the time, my family never stood in my way. I had a good background and a secure home. They're a very straight family but they are wise and they weren't against me. They're good people, and they'd had kids before. My brother's thirty-seven and he was a biker before, and my sister's thirty. So they'd seen that kids were going to do what they were going to do. I still ring them up once a week to see how they are, because mothers worry. I try and discourage them from visiting me on site, because there are certain aspects of site life I wouldn't want them to be exposed to. They've sheltered themselves and I don't feel it's my duty to expose them to things like drunkenness and violence.

A lot of it's boredom. People get bored and they drink and they've got an attitude against the whole system. If people say 'Stand up,' they want to sit down, whether it's a good idea or not. It's really down to the pressures. Before, people were a lot mellower. There's a lot of anger everywhere today. People are very angry about what's going on. You never see '500 jobs to be created next week' on the news, do you? Employers can pay anything they want, so if you're willing to work for £40 a week . . .

When we first started I felt we were turning people on to something, taking people from cardboard boxes on to sites, giving them homes. The reform of the Caravan Sites Act that they're proposing is part of a policy. They want everyone in concrete boxes or cardboard boxes. Once you're in a cardboard box there's nothing for you. There's a section of society that would say gas 'em if they thought they could get away with it. Good old England. It's a very cold country at the moment.

A lot of people will do this for ever, they'll fight the establishment for ever. But then the bottom line as far as I can see is if you live your life as a traveller you either end up in prison or you're forced abroad.

But I don't think I'm disillusioned. I'm more content now than when I was fighting, banging my head against it. There's truth and there's good and evil. I'd like to think I stand on the side of good, but there's got to be a system. I've changed my attitude towards it. There's too many people in this world now not to be a system. There's got to be an authority.

Privacy has a lot to do with why I want to leave, thinking about it now. Anything you do on site everyone knows about. You get your privacy in your own home behind your doors but there is a lack of privacy, definitely.

And I'm bored of it.

We've got a couple of numbers of houses to ring up tomorrow. It'll be easy living in a house. Maybe too easy. I expect I'll get bored, but I want to give it a go. Ideally, I'd like to buy an old cottage and do it up. I won't have to go on a water run or go wooding, which is good.

You can use my full name if you want. Years ago I would have been paranoid about you using it, but I haven't done anything I'm ashamed of. Don Charman: ex-traveller.

I don't know . . . will I like living in a house? If it all goes wrong, in two weeks' time I'd have a ratty old motor and a caravan, I'd have a fire going, I could offer you a cup of tea.

Like I say, sometimes I have a couple of beers, listen to the right tape and it brings it all back again.

No regrets, me. Life's too short.

SHANNON

It's the end of the road for Shannon. He's been travelling for fifteen years now, since he was fifteen: Britain, America, India, all over the Far East, Australia, Ibiza. He's been there. He's done it all. But the game's up. It was his beloved green van that got him into trouble; his pride and joy that he'd spent months fitting out; his home while he's been travelling in Wales and England. He'd parked it outside his friend's house in North London in November 1992. He didn't realise the police had cordoned off the area and were scouring it for IRA bombs. Strange green vans look suspicious when you're the bomb squad sniffing out terrorist explosives. And if it's your van, and it contains half a kilo of hash, you're in the soup.

The hash was going to pay Shannon's way to India and then on to Spain for the winter. Instead, it landed him in Pentonville, where he had to eat soggy beans on toast and veg with the life boiled out of them and think seriously about his future. Unless he could prove to the magistrates that he was going to change his ways and embark on something constructive, he'd probably go down for a year. He was thirty. It was time for a change. He made a decision. He was going to put his experience and his ideals to good use – go to college and study environmental science, so that he could put his ideas into practice instead of just talking about them.

So here he is, holed up in a bail hostel in Catford for three months awaiting trial. The van will have to go to pay for the courses he wants to take. All that work he put into it and he'll have to sell it cheap – it's a buyer's market in January.

All in all it's a disaster. But Shannon believes in fate. He believes things happen for a reason. Even the bad things.

I can look on it as really unfortunate or look on it as a blessing, a kick in the arse to get something together. If I hadn't had this slap in the face I probably would have dragged on for years drifting around doing nothing.

Maybe it's an age thing too; I know a lot of travellers that get to around thirty and start taking stock a bit, but there's no compromise on my part. I'm not getting cosy and conformist with age. But you either ignore it, or bang your head against the wall or actually decide to do something about it.

I don't want to buy a house and a car and get a straight job and live in Milton Keynes. I'm as against that as I ever was. My hate for the police, my hate for the government, my hate for the plastic impersonal world that I was brought up in was really strong and raging when I was young. Now I'm calmer about it – I know it's going to go on with or without me and raging against it is only going to cause trouble for me.

In Australia I was involved in a lot of illegal subversive environmental work – I'd be in the Australian bush, see this beautiful vista, with nature and harmony and then suddenly this fucking great big fifty-foot billboard for a fucking Kenwood mixer or something. I'd just get a chainsaw and tear it down. I loved doing things like that.

But the only thing I thought was any real use was when I was working on building sites and educating carpenters on what woods to buy and what woods to avoid, the ones which are from regenerated forests as opposed to Malaysian prime rainforests. But that's just a scratch compared to what I could do if I pursue this. When I was sitting in prison thinking about getting an education, thinking about my future, there were four things which I thought of that were not being hit by recession, that were always going to be thriving. One is drug dealing because people are taking more drugs than ever before. I don't want to do that any more – I can't afford to. Another is law because more people are getting caught dealing drugs, but I'm not inclined to that. The other is psychotherapy because everyone's getting more fucked up and they know about it. I'm not really drawn into that even though I find it quite interesting. The only other expanding area I can think of is the environment, caring for the planet, and that's something that I care about and really attracts me.

Drugs is an epidemic, a frightening one really. I've been dealing hash for years. But I wouldn't touch heroin or crack. I could have made a great deal of money dealing heroin over the years but I wouldn't touch it. I see a massive difference between that and hash. Smack is a soul-destroying drug, it eats people. Crack and cocaine are almost as bad; they get more important to the user than anything else, more important than friendships. Hash is nothing like that, it's less dangerous than alcohol, not as pointless as cigarettes, not particularly healthy but definitely not damaging.

The business I was doing with it I thought was pretty constructive really. I was giving money to Third World farmers in the Indian Himalayas. The money was not taxed so it went direct to them and their families. They put it right back into the earth and it kept them alive. I brought a product which didn't harm anybody to Britain and people enjoyed using it. I felt really good about that. It wasn't taxed, no nasty bankers or governments getting their hands on the money to do things I don't approve of and I felt good about it. Hash doesn't kill people, it might just about give someone a cough. I did enough to support myself, to make the odd couple of grand here and there, to live in the West for a while and go back to India when I needed to or wanted to.

I still remember my first experience of the travellers' scene really clearly. When I was fifteen I got in trouble and my mum sent me to America to stay with an uncle for a while. I ended up staying there a couple of years, playing in punk bands in LA. Just after I got back from there – this must have been 1980 – I heard about this mushroom festival in Wales. Me and my girlfriend hitched up there with about £1.50 between us.

We caught a ride with some hippies who were going to the festival. I remember the scene even now. We came round a corner and there was like a west-facing valley with pine trees coming down and a flat bottom, the sun setting at the end of the valley. At the bottom of the valley there were all these teepees and benders with smoke rising out of the top of them. It looked like some picture of the Rocky Mountains in Colorado hundreds of years ago. The pine trees, the teepees, the sunset, it was gorgeous. It was something totally new to me – people living in benders, spending the whole year in them, just tarpaulin and rugs and cloth, trying to live in a way totally different from society. And the energy it had to it then was extraordinary.

Someone said, 'Build a bender,' and I didn't know what it was so they showed me and we made one out of plastic. Later on we got some tarpaulin. We stayed there about two weeks, still with just that £1.50 between us. I was seventeen at the time and she was maybe sixteen and people just looked after us and fed us and gave us ganga to smoke and just welcomed us totally.

When you go to a festival now and it's just full-on Buy Buy, Sell Sell, Drugs Drugs – it wasn't like that then. I remember there was this guy with a massive kettle who just sat by this fire making cups of tea for everyone. Everybody who walked past his bender he went 'Cup of tea? Cup of tea?' – nowadays of course it's 50p in a polystyrene cup – so you'd sit down and have a cup of tea and a chat. He just got off on talking to people and the tea was his contribution to the scene. You'd sit and chat and spliff up and give him a spliff in exchange for his cup of tea and that was the scene there. Money was really scowled upon. People didn't really like to deal with money. Some of that does remain with the travellers' sites now – there's still that love of trading things, bartering, which people are still really into. I suppose it was impossible for it to continue in the idealistic way as it got bigger.

It sounds like I'm being really down on the travelling scene of today and praising how it was ten years ago, moaning about how things have changed for the worse. In a way I am, personally, but looking on it objectively, I think travellers and the travelling scene is going to play a really big part in the future of British society.

I don't know how many thousands, maybe hundreds of thousands, are living like this but it's going to get bigger. Next year, the year after maybe, it'll be as many as half a million. That's a large section of society. It's a lot of people to try and sweep away and put out of view. It's an army of people who don't give a shit about law and order, who don't give a shit about society, about washing machines, about three-piece suites, mortgages and flash cars, which is what this society is based on: the hunger to have the so-called good things, to have your microwaves, your new Sierras. What are they going to do when there's such a huge section of society not falling for that?

Materialism is the new opium of the people – it keeps everyone going to work so they can pay their mortgage and buy all these things. That consumerism is being rejected by a massive amount of people. Not necessarily in a positive way. A lot of travellers I know don't give a fuck for anything beyond the next can of Special Brew. But from society's point of view it's dangerous. It's a big force of people who aren't scared, even if it comes to conflict. They've been in nick, they've been beaten up by police, they've had the bad side of all that – they've got nothing to lose apart from a twenty-quid caravan and a few bits and bobs.

I don't think it's something which can be just brushed under the mat. I think for a lot of people in establishment positions it's something they've got very good reason to be scared of. Travellers aren't that much of a danger in reality – they're a slight nuisance maybe, they might shoplift a bit, they might nick stuff out of farmyards – but they are a big threat to what is considered British and normal.

People covered in filth, wearing ragged clothes, drinking cans of Special Brew and hanging round begging in shopping malls is not considered to be a part of modern Britain, where nobody's supposed to starve, where nobody's supposed to be homeless, where everybody has their opportunity for their car and their washing machine, and this hurts people. It makes people scared and uneasy. It's part of the modern world they'd rather didn't exist. And I think deep down, underneath, a lot of these people realise that this country is going downhill economically and socially, getting really bad, but they'd rather not look under Waterloo Bridge, they'd rather not go to the housing estates in Tottenham. Most people don't want to be reminded of what the real situation is. It frightens them.

And who can blame the travellers for rejecting the society they live in? When I live in London and look around I see miserable shell-suit-clad people living in sterile worlds. They never get their hands in the earth, they never saw bits of firewood, they've never washed themselves in a cold stream or anything like that. They live in a world of TV, video games, Ford Sierras and getting their little semi-detached house.

To have the feeling of not knowing where I'm going next, not knowing where my food is coming from next and having the freedom to do pretty much what I want makes me feel alive, makes me feel I really am an individual person. Living a life that I choose to do, not living a life that has been set out for me because it's been accepted as the right thing to do. I can moan a hell of a lot about the lack of care and the ignorance of some travellers, but something inside me is really happy to see so many more people going that way. There's kids who have never ever been out of a city that I've met on sites who've just one day got on a bus or got on a bicycle or started hitching and never ever gone back to Tottenham or Brixton or wherever it is they came from and just found a new lease of life, found something new in themselves. Most people look so bloody miserable. And I think a lot of the hatred of travellers is out of envy. They're jealous of people having a free easy life without the drudgery of a soul-destroying job.

I see more life on a travellers' site than I see on the street in London. A lot more joy in being alive, a lot more excitement, a lot more spark for life. Even though there's so much alcoholism, so much drug abuse, the side that pisses me off. But youth everywhere, in the cities, in rural areas, are getting into drugs in a very big way now.

And I think some of the energy of the travellers' scene of ten years ago is still there. People genuinely trying to live an alternative life: keeping goats rather than buying milk in cartons, not signing on and having their living supplemented by society but doing crafts, art, travelling round the vegetable-picking and fruit-picking areas, getting farm work and stuff like that.

I don't think it should be a crime to want to live like that, to want to live in a rural area rather than a big city. And it's impossible to go out and rent a cottage or a farmhouse or buy one. Apart from people who are born to it, rural Britain is for the rich. It's for people who can afford to buy themselves a weekend place or go and retire in the country. For me, if I want to live with space around me and trees and hills and woods, the only possible way apart from sleeping out is to buy a vehicle and live in that.

In the early days I would park up by myself. The phenomenon of sites is fairly recent. In the old days you could find a little lane or a bit of field and park up by yourself. Now you always get moved off places like that and there's not really much else to do but go on sites. When I came back to Britain I wanted to avoid being part of the travellers' scene; just wanted to live on my own, but I ended up having to live on sites because they were the only places to go. It's part of the reason I've decided I don't want to travel any more in this country. Sites can be terrible. Dogs, kids and filth. Smack and alcohol. All that's definitely getting worse as a result of more people getting involved in travelling. Whereas in the early eighties it was mostly alternative-y type people who picked an alternative lifestyle, now it's people who are basically fucked off with the city. In a way that's made it more unpleasant. It's not the rosy rainbow hippie scene it was in the seventies and eighties, people trying to live in love and peace. It's not that. But that isn't going to exist in the nineties. Society is cruel and it's horrible and these people are products of it. They're going to have to be recognised as part of this world and allowed to live the way they live or there's going to be massive confrontation. I've heard so many stories of violence against travellers – just six weeks or so ago where I was staying in Wales somebody drove past and emptied a shotgun into somebody's caravan; probably a local farmer.

Abroad it's a different scene. The scene I've been into in the past ten years has been what I call the international travellers, people who go to Goa every year, people who go to Japan to work for two months or do the circuit of India, Thailand, Bali and Japan, Ibiza. This has been my scene and my family, a world-wide tribe. There's people I've known for ten years in India, people who come back year after year. It's completely international, although some of the British people were once travellers in Britain – there's German, French, American, Australian, Dutch, Italians. Goa's on the west coast of India, south of Bombay and it's been a hippie haunt since the sixties – beautiful beaches. I've been there every winter for seven years bar one and it's as much my home as anywhere. I was going back there a week ago until I got busted. There's a whole group of people going right from jet-setters who were born rich and just spend their money going to Goa and Thailand and places like that, right down to crossovers from the British travellers' scene.

It's an easy life. You can live in luxury on twenty quid a week. A lot of the people I hang around with are second generationers. Me too, I was in India when I was a kid with my mum. She's there now at the moment meditating – good on her. I lived there for a while when my dad was in the navy – probably why my mum split up with him. I haven't seen him in ten years. He may well be one of the people I'll be legally fighting against. He's a geophysicist, .

involved in all kinds of lovely stuff, probably, like strip-mining uranium, ripping off the Third World for their natural resources.

India's been more my home than anywhere and it's weird for me planning to go to college for three years and breaking away from what's been my family for ten years. A lot of them go to Japan – the girls sing in the bars or waitress or do escort work and the guys usually run hash, that's one of the biggest ways of making money for the international travellers. That's how I've financed going to India for the last few years, running hash.

I've had a fucking good run for my money, I suppose. I've spent years in Asia, Europe, Australia, places most people have never even been. I've had a lucky time. I came back last year for a couple of months. I got ripped off in India last year, lost all my money and got a cheap flight back to England. I did some business, non-legal, that got me a couple of grand when I arrived and I just wanted to buy a truck, drive up to the Welsh mountains and live like a caveman. I was a bit sick of everybody. I wanted to just make my dal and chapatis, sit by my fire at night and play the guitar and not be hassled by anybody or see anyone if I didn't want to. I did that for a few months.

Come June I'd had enough of being left alone so I went and done the festivals. I met up with people I'd not seen for years and years, got back in the travellers' scene and lived on sites and stuff. Good festivals this year. Castlemorton was amazing, just unruly, complete anarchy. The festival was like an animal. I got up on the hill and looked down on all the people at night and it was like this big writhing beast.

The rave scene has made the festies very different. It's a funny crossover considering a lot of the old travellers are into acoustic music and bongos and Irish music or whatever. It's funny that it's seen as a new thing though, because that's been done in Goa for years. By 1982, 1983, people there were using electronic house music, early bands like Yello, Kraftwerk, Cabaret Voltaire, New Order and mixing over stuff like that with Hendrix and Deep

Purple and making real collages of music, all with an electronic beat and everybody taking acid, wearing fluorescent clothes and dancing all night. Bloody beautiful. That's why they say all the acid house scene started in Ibiza, because it spread from Goa to Ibiza with the international travellers' scene.

Arriving back in Britain after a few years and seeing all these raves was weird, especially it merging with the old travellers' scene which I knew already. I don't really like them though, compared to the Goa scene – too aggressive really. I remember reading about the '87, '88 acid house scene in Britain when I was in Australia and India and thinking, 'Wey, hey, they've caught on at last, it's what we've been doing on the beach for the past four or five years.' But that's ruined Goa in a way – the past couple of years you've had all these British ravers, which is kind of verging on the football hooligan type of people and mentality, and they've spoiled it a bit.

It's time to move on. I'll still be a traveller – it's in my blood – but if I've got this degree places like South America and Asia are just going to open up to me in a new way. I can go there and instead of being an onlooker – looking at India and how industrialism is ruining that place and the air in Bombay is completely unbreathable; instead of just looking at it and being sad about it – I can actually go and do things. I've been running on luck for the last fifteen years; it's time to stop drifting, to change the way I work in the world. It's time to get my shit together.

Acknowledgments

Richard Lowe and William Shaw would like to thank all of those who helped us to put this book together in such a short space of time. Among those whose advice and knowledge were invaluable were Ann Bagehot of Save The Children, David Gosling, Ian Cairns, Chris Gilham, Jane Sand and Jane Irwine from the West Penwith Travellers Support Group, Richard Cotterill and the Travellers School Charity, Paul Simmonds, Chloe, Bella, Tim Everson Naomi Lowe, Grace Pachman and Jane Carr. We'd also like to thank Jane McMorrow for her interviews and transcriptions. Finally, we're especially grateful to all the many travellers up and down the country who invited us into their vehicles, trailers and benders, plied us with endless cups of tea, and gave up hours of their time answering our questions.